"What? This is a cookbook? A cookbook! I remember when they first started making cookbooks. I HATE THEM!"

—Baby Prunes

"ME HOY MINOY WABAWABA!!!!"

—DoodleBob

THE OFFICIAL SPONGEBOB SQUAREPANTS™ COOKBOOK

FAVORITE DISHES FROM YOUR FRIENDS IN BIKINI BOTTOM

THE OFFICIAL SPONGEBOB SQUAREPANTS™ COOKBOOK

OVER 50 TREASURED RECIPES FROM UNDER THE SEA

Recipes developed by Jarrett Melendez
Food photography by Leela Cyd

TEN SPEED PRESS
California | New York

nickelodeon

CONTENTS

Jellyfish
Fields

INTRODUCTION

A LETTER FROM THE BIKINI BOTTOM HISTORICAL SOCIETY

Greetings, Bikini Bottomites from the future!

I'm Ms. Mayor—president and founding member of the Bikini Bottom Historical Society. What you hold in your hands/tentacles/fins/flippers is the culmination of years of work that we, the BBHS, have worked toward: a culinary time capsule of all the tastes of Bikini Bottom.

Cooking and sharing meals are part of how a community comes together. It's a way to connect to one another. Sure, everybody has to eat. But what we choose to eat, what brings us comfort, and what makes us smile say a lot about who we are.

That's why we're putting this cookbook together! We wanted to take a snapshot of what our fellow citizens of Bikini Bottom are eating *right now* and preserve those recipes to be immortalized throughout all of time and space, in perpetuity throughout the universe! That's right, folks. This cookbook is a bona fide piece of Bikini Bottom history filled with recipes from our most notable (and in some cases, *infamous*) citizens and historical figures in the making, and it will live in the collection at the Historical Society for our great-great-great-grandkids and other random strangers to enjoy forever.

Within this tome, you can expect to find recipes for such delicacies as Sandy Cheeks's Hot Crossed Nuts (page 20), Patrick Star Pastina (page 78), Larry the Lobster's Protein Shake (page 158), and . . . reader, are you ready for this? In this very book, we will finally reveal one of Bikini Bottom's most closely guarded secrets. That's right, we will finally reveal the actual, real, totally authentic, utterly verified recipe for . . . the Krabby Patty!

So, fire up the stove and warm up your stirring arm because when you cook from our cookbook, *you're* part of Bikini Bottom history too!

THE BIKINI BOTTOM HISTORICAL SOCIETY

Ms. Mayor, *President*

SpongeBob SquarePants, *Vice President, Treasurer, Secretary, Under Secretary, Bursar, Registrar, Comptroller, and Chimney Sweep*

EQUIPMENT & INGREDIENTS

This list of totally essential kitchen gadgets, doohickeys, and thingamabobs has been vetted by the townsfish of Bikini Bottom for use for the most delicious results when making their recipes (and some more pedestrian alternatives, as needed).

Anti-Sea-Rhinoceros Undergarments: Wear these anytime you're cooking to keep sea rhinoceroses out of your kitchen. While these specialized undergarments are an optional tool, be prepared to deal with the consequences of a sea rhinoceros infestation if you decide not to don them. Or simply use a kitchen apron for coverage.

Canned Coral: Tired of harvesting your own coral from the local reef? Well, now it comes in convenient cans! There's no substitute for the fresh stuff, but canned coral does well in a pinch and gives you that satisfying crunch you crave.

Chum: Who *knows* what this actually is or how it's used. We asked Plankton, and although he's a culinary . . . well, *genius* isn't the word we're looking for. Culinary impresario? Culinary prodigy? Culinary Megalomaniacal Menace! Yes, we asked Plankton the Culinary Megalomaniacal Menace about chum and he didn't know what's in it either. Anyway, don't cook with chum, it's gross.

Drinkable Sausage: Sold by the carton, each container contains approximately 17⅓ sausages in liquid, drinkable form. All the flavor of sausage with none of the texture! Wow!

Fully Automated Nutcracker: Used to crack nuts, this device will make short work of those pesky shells keeping you from enjoying delicious nuts. If you don't have one, simply buying shelled nuts will do.

YUMMY STUFF
YUMMY STUFF
YUMMY STUFF
YUMMY STUFF
YUMMY STUFF
YUMMY STUFF
YUMMY STUFF
YUMMY STUFF
YUMMY STUFF

Ghost Catcher 5000: We've found that this handy device is perfect when you're looking to round up some guests for a last-minute dinner party. It will catch any ghosts, ghouls, poltergeists, and/or specters in a snap. You'll make a new friend, and it's always handy to have a buddy who can pass through walls or reach for that spice jar in the back of the cabinet.

Golden Spatula: You'll need this to flip burgers, shift cookies from the pan to a cooling rack, and other menial tasks. You *can* use a regular spatula to perform these moves, but keep in mind that your food won't taste quite the same. It'll taste *exactly* the same.

Iron Butt: A great thing to keep around in case you severely injure your butt while preparing any of these recipes or while carrying on with your day-to-day activities in this funny little thing we call life. In the event that you do injure your butt, we wish you a speedy recovery. May you and your butt bounce back stronger than ever. If you don't have access to an Iron Butt, please consult your nearest medical professional.

Knockout Ray: This proved very helpful as we were gathering the recipes for this collection. We used it to knock out Plankton, who did provide some recipes for this book, every time he got a little too close to getting the recipe for the Krabby Patty (page 81). Of course, now that we've published that recipe here, perhaps all that knocking out of Plankton was pointless. Anyway, use this against snoops trying to steal your secret recipes.

Laser Helmet: Great for heating up leftovers or preventing people from stepping on you. Fred asks that you keep away from him if you insist on using one, however.

Mermaid Man and Barnacle Boy's Time Machine: Professional chefs don't want you to know about this time-saving hack. Simply prepare a dish as directed, then take it with you back in time to when you started making the dish. Boom. Time saved. *Warning*: Using this hack may cause a rift in the time-space continuum that keeps you in an endless loop of the same five minutes and/or tears apart the very fabric of reality like a tissue at a snot party. Results may vary (see page 97 for a delicious result!).

Mrs. Puff Robot: A fantastic option to use for making your Mrs. Puff's Cream Puffs (page 133). The robot comes preprogrammed with the recipe. Just switch her on, ask for a batch, and set her loose in your kitchen. If you don't have one, you'll have to make the cream puffs yourself. Sorry!

Powdered Driftwood: Ever have one of those dishes that has a certain *je ne sais quois*? There's a 0.0000001 percent chance that the *quois* you *je ne sais* is powdered driftwood! And, frankly, we love those odds. Try some on your next dish for that nummy yummy driftwoody goodness.

Rare Fruit of the Kazook Tree: A foul stench beyond compare, but when you combine this rare, expensive fruit with the even rarer and more expensive shredded gold, it neutralizes its odor and you get something completely indescribable. It's expensive, so it's gotta be good!

Seahorse Radish: Despite the picture on the jar, we want the Bikini Bottomites of the future to know that this is not made from real seahorses. It is, according to SpongeBob, the gnarliest stuff in the ocean.

Sonic Cannon That Destroys Every Known Material in the Universe: As the name suggests, this piece of equipment will destroy any dish you make, along with you, your kitchen, and, well, everything. So, it's not so much that you need this to make anything in this cookbook, but you should know where yours is at all times to avoid accidental eradication of everything you hold dear. If you don't have one, good! A handy compost container can work just as well.

MENU SUGGESTIONS

Here at the Bikini Bottom Historical Society, we believe that food is best shared with friends and family of all stripes, spots, fins, and flippers. Here are a few different menu ideas we put together for you to use at your next gathering.

PICNIC AT SEASHELL PARK

Hot Crossed Nuts (page 20)

Spicy Pineapple Cheeseball (page 24)

King Neptune's Spears (page 70)

Coco-Hut Salad (page 101)

Ink Lemonade (page 148)

SQUIDWARD'S DINNER PARTY

Canned Bread (page 28)

Sea Pebble Stew (page 53)

5-Star Alfredo (page 56)

Double Dark Deep Sea Cake (page 111)

The Bikini Bottom (page 154)

BARBECUE AT SANDY'S

Chips and Grilled Pineapple Salsa (page 21)

Golden Loaf (page 27)

Mac and Cheese Pie (page 51)

Sandy's Texas-Style Chili con Carne (page 65)

Sandy's Texas Sheet Cake (page 102)

Pineapple Under the Sea (page 144)

DINNER AT PLANKTON'S

Diabolically Delicious Deviled Eggs (page 35)

Holographic Meat Loaf (page 63)

Coconut Green Beans (page 77)

Kerglooginpfiefer mit Schlusinberry Klabber Sauz (page 129)

Fizzy Fang (page 157)

BEST FRIENDS FOREVER PARTY WITH SPONGEBOB AND PATRICK

Chicken Chorizo Nachos (page 37)

Wiener Takes All (page 55)

Triple Gooberberry Sunrise (page 119)

Mini Pineapple Upside-Down Cakes (page 127)

Patrick's Pink Punch (page 153)

CHAPTER ONE

APPETIZERS

APPETIZERS

Cookbooks (and, well, all books!) have to start somewhere, and to that, every meal has to start somewhere: the beginning! So, let's begin by beginning.

Who doesn't love a moment for a snack? There are so many wonderful snacks and appetizers out there. In this chapter, you'll find all kinds of tasty treats meant to whet appetites big and small, like Sandy Cheeks's Hot Crossed Nuts (page 20; these little beauties are so delicious that they took the Krusty Krab by storm and almost put SpongeBob out of a job!) and the glowing green snack that gave Mermaid Man and Barnacle Boy their powers, Radioactive Popcorn (page 32), which probably won't give *you* powers but is still tasty!

If you're planning a party, you might like to pass around some appetizers to fill up your guests' little plates, empty stomachs, and, of course, those awkward silences that tend to happen when big groups of people are forced to make small talk. Keep their jaws occupied with dishes like the Weenie Hut Jr. Tot Sliders (page 23) or Diabolically Delicious Deviled Eggs (page 35). Then your guests will have something *interesting* to talk about—how good the food is—instead of carrying on about how their aunt's dog's dentist's cousin's paleontologist's kid's little league game went.

Read on for tropical-inspired, pineapple-laden delicious delights like Lady Upturn's Spicy Pineapple Cheeseball (page 24) or Harold and Margaret SquarePants's Pineapple Under the Sea-zza (page 42). Fish of the future, for reasons I am not entirely sure of, pineapple on pizza is divisive and controversial. As mayor, I represent everyone in Bikini Bottom and everyone's taste buds are welcome. Unless it's chum pizza. Then, well, no.

SEA PICKLE CHIPS

CONTRIBUTED BY FLATS THE FLOUNDER

We just love these tangy little pickle chips from Flats the Flounder. He tells us that all you need to do is slice up some cukes and soak them in a brine that's about as briny as the briny deep but with *flavor*. Sea Pickle Chips make a tasty snack all on their own, but you can use them to add a burst of tangy goodness to any burger, including the Weenie Hut Jr. Tot Sliders on page 23. They could even be a key component to the legendary Krabby Patty! Could Flats the Flounder truly hold such a foundational secret? We'll never tell!

MAKES ABOUT 1 QUART

8 ounces seedless mini cucumbers (such as Persian or Kirby), trimmed and sliced ¼ inch thick

1 cup distilled white vinegar

1 cup water

2 teaspoons kosher salt

1½ teaspoons yellow mustard seeds

1 teaspoon black peppercorns

2 garlic cloves, smashed

3 sprigs dill

1. Put the cucumber slices into a 1-quart mason jar. Set aside.
2. In a small saucepan, combine the vinegar, water, and salt. Bring to a boil over high heat, stirring occasionally until the salt dissolves. Stir in the mustard seeds and peppercorns and remove from the heat.
3. Add the garlic and dill to the jar with the cucumbers. Pour the hot vinegar mixture over the cucumbers, submerging them. Let sit, uncovered, for 30 minutes. Cap the jar tightly and refrigerate for at least 4 hours before serving. The pickle chips will keep in the fridge for up to 1 month.

HOT CROSSED NUTS

CONTRIBUTED BY SANDY CHEEKS

If you want a bunch of nuts packed with tasty barbecue flavor, Sandy Cheeks has got a recipe for you. Passed down through generations of squirrels from Texas, this recipe comes from Sandy's great-great-granny Cheeks! The secret to this recipe is to use whatever ratio of nuts you like. If you like only almonds, use just almonds! If you like cashews and pecans, use those! Customize to your heart's desire.

MAKES 3½ CUPS

¼ cup lightly packed light brown sugar

1 tablespoon smoked paprika

1 teaspoon kosher salt

1 teaspoon ancho chile powder

1 teaspoon ground mustard

½ teaspoon ground cumin

½ teaspoon ground coriander

½ teaspoon freshly ground black pepper

1 egg white

3½ cups mixed raw nuts (such as pecans, pistachios, cashews, and almonds)

1. Preheat the oven to 325°F. Line a half sheet pan with parchment paper.
2. In a large bowl, whisk together the sugar, paprika, salt, chile powder, mustard, cumin, coriander, and pepper until well mixed.
3. In a small bowl, using a fork, beat the egg white until frothy. Add to the bowl with the spice mixture and stir until mixed. Add the nuts to the egg white–spice mixture and, using a rubber spatula, carefully stir and fold in the nuts until they are evenly coated.
4. Pour the nuts onto the prepared sheet pan and spread in a single layer. Bake the nuts, stirring every 10 to 15 minutes, until toasted and almost completely dry, 45 to 60 minutes. If you're unsure if the nuts are ready, carefully scoop a few out of the pan, drop them onto a small plate, and let cool for a few minutes. Then taste them, and if they're dry and crunchy, the nuts are ready. Let the nuts cool on the pan on a wire cooling rack to room temperature.
5. Transfer the nuts to an airtight container. They will keep at room temperature for up to 3 weeks.

CHIPS AND GRILLED PINEAPPLE SALSA

CONTRIBUTED BY SCOOTER

From a surfer bro's mind to your dinner table, Scooter's Chips and Grilled Pineapple Salsa is sure to satisfy. "Let me let *you* in on a little secret, dude," he tells us in a whisper. "Fire plus pineapple equals awwwwwesooooome." We took that to mean, of course, that by cooking the pineapple over an open flame, you caramelize some of the sugars, enhancing the pineapple's natural sweetness, while also adding a touch of smokiness that carries through to the final dish. We think.

SERVES 4 TO 6

½ small pineapple, peeled, cut crosswise into ½-inch-thick slices, and slices cored (about 4 slices)

2 tablespoons neutral oil (such as canola or safflower oil)

4 plum tomatoes, cored and diced

1 small red onion, diced

1 serrano chile, seeded and minced

½ teaspoon kosher salt, plus more as needed

½ teaspoon Tajín seasoning or chili powder

¼ teaspoon ground coriander

Juice of 1 lime

Leaves from ½ bunch cilantro, coarsely chopped

Tortilla chips, for serving

1. Prepare a charcoal or gas grill for direct-heat cooking over high heat. Alternatively, position an oven rack 4 to 6 inches from the heat source and preheat the broiler. Line a sheet pan with aluminum foil for easier cleanup.
2. Pat the pineapple slices dry with paper towels, then brush each slice on both sides with the oil. To grill the slices, place them on the grill racks directly over the fire and grill, turning once, until lightly charred with grill marks on both sides, 2 to 3 minutes on each side. To broil the slices, arrange them in a single layer on the prepared sheet pan, place under the broiler, and broil, turning once, until golden brown on both sides, 2 to 3 minutes on each side. Broiler strength can vary, so watch closely to prevent burning.
3. Transfer the grilled pineapple to a cutting board and let cool until cool enough to handle. Cut into coarse dice and transfer to a medium bowl along with any accumulated juices.
4. Add the tomatoes, onion, chile, salt, Tajín, coriander, lime juice, and cilantro to the bowl holding the pineapple and toss and stir to combine. Taste and adjust the seasoning with salt if needed.
5. Cover and refrigerate for about 1 hour before serving, then serve with tortilla chips. Leftover salsa will keep in an airtight container in the fridge for up to 5 days.

WEENIE HUT JR. TOT SLIDERS

CONTRIBUTED BY WEENIE HUT JR.

When we asked the robot employee from Weenie Hut Jr. if it would be possible to get a recipe for this book, it printed this recipe out then called us all a bunch of weenies. When we wrote to corporate headquarters to complain, we got back the following:

Dear Valued Customer, We are sorry our Weenie Bot called you a weenie, you weenie. To compensate you for your trouble, we are sending you a coupon for 1 percent off your next order. It will arrive in six to eight business years. You weenie.

Anyway, these tot sliders are great with Flats the Flounder's homemade Sea Pickle Chips (page 19), but store-bought pickle chips work well too.

SERVES 4 TO 6

24 tater rounds

8 ounces 90 percent lean ground beef or plant-based ground meat alternative

½ teaspoon kosher salt

¼ teaspoon freshly ground black pepper

2 tablespoons neutral oil (such as canola or safflower)

2 slices American cheese, cut into 24 equal pieces each about ¾ inch square

6 pickle chips, homemade (page 19) or store-bought, each cut into 4 wedges

Ketchup, for dipping

Mustard, for dipping

1. Cook the tater rounds according to the package directions. Once they have finished cooking, keep them warm until you are ready to build the sliders.
2. While the tater rounds cook, cut two pieces of parchment paper, each about 8 square inches. Lay one piece on a work surface, set the beef in the center, and top with the second parchment sheet. Using a rolling pin, roll out the beef into a 6-inch square. Peel off the top sheet of parchment and season the beef with the salt and pepper.
3. Cut the beef square into twenty-four 1 by 1½-inch rectangles. In a large skillet over medium heat, warm the oil. When the oil is shimmering, add the beef rectangles in a single layer and cook until well seared on the underside and almost cooked through, 3 to 4 minutes. Flip the mini burgers and remove the pan from the heat. The residual heat will be enough to cook them through.
4. Top each mini burger with a piece of cheese and a wedge of pickle. Place a dressed burger on top of each warm tater round, then pierce each slider with a toothpick to secure the burger. Transfer the sliders to a serving platter and serve with ketchup and mustard for dipping.

SPICY PINEAPPLE CHEESEBALL

CONTRIBUTED BY LADY UPTURN

This fancy little cheeseball, which gets a kick of spice from smoky chipotle chile powder, comes to us from the illustrious Lady Upturn. We were so grateful she deigned to grace us with a recipe from her housekeeper and thought it was adorable that the end product looks a bit like Patrick Star's house. When we asked if this was on purpose or just a happy coincidence, she looked aghast, stormed off, and shouted, "I am offended!"

SERVES 4 TO 6

One 8-ounce package cream cheese, at room temperature

6 ounces pepper Jack cheese, shredded

¼ teaspoon chipotle chile powder, plus more as needed

½ cup crushed pineapple, well drained

1 jarred roasted red bell pepper, drained and diced

½ cup chopped toasted pecans

Crackers, carrot sticks, and/or celery sticks, for serving

1. In a food processor, combine the cream cheese and pepper Jack and process until smooth and creamy, stopping to scrape down the sides of the bowl with a rubber spatula as needed. Add the chile powder and process until well mixed. Taste and adjust the seasoning with more chile powder if needed.
2. Using the spatula, scrape the cheese mixture into a medium bowl. Add the pineapple and red pepper and fold in until evenly distributed. Cover the bowl with plastic wrap and refrigerate for about 1 hour to firm up.
3. With gloved hands, scoop the cheese mixture from the bowl and roughly shape into a ball. Place the ball on a medium serving platter and gently press down on the top to create a rough half-sphere shape, then continue to shape and smooth the half-sphere with an offset spatula.
4. Cover the surface of the cheeseball evenly with the pecans, pressing them gently so they adhere. Serve with crackers and/or vegetable sticks.

GOLDEN LOAF

CONTRIBUTED BY MERMAID MAN AND BARNACLE BOY

This recipe comes straight from your favorite golden-age crime-fighting duo, Mermaid Man and Barnacle Boy. Here's what they had to say about the origin: "Origin?! Aw, everyone knows that," said Mermaid Man. "Y'see, it all started with this batch of radioactive popcorn and me and—" Mermaid Man carried on like this for some time, starting and stopping stories that didn't seem to have anything to do with each other. Eventually, Barnacle Boy interrupted and told us that he was the one who came up with the whipped honey butter, then grumbled at length about how Mermaid Man never gave him credit for anything . . . So there you have it, folks—a lovely cornbread and a fine accompaniment to Sandy's Texas-Style Chili con Carne (page 65).

MAKES ONE 9 BY 5-INCH LOAF

CORNBREAD

- 1½ cups fine yellow cornmeal
- 1 cup all-purpose flour
- 2 teaspoons baking powder
- 1½ teaspoons kosher salt
- ½ cup unsalted butter, melted and cooled
- 2 eggs
- 1 cup canned cream-style corn
- ¼ cup honey
- ¼ cup buttermilk

WHIPPED HONEY BUTTER

- ½ cup unsalted butter, at room temperature
- 3 tablespoons honey
- 2 teaspoons kosher salt
- 1 teaspoon ground cinnamon

1. To make the cornbread: Preheat the oven to 350°F. Butter a 9 by 5-inch loaf pan.
2. In a medium bowl, whisk together the cornmeal, flour, baking powder, and salt. Set aside.
3. In a large bowl, whisk together the melted butter and eggs until smooth. Add the cream-style corn and stir until blended, then stir in the honey and buttermilk, mixing well. Add the cornmeal mixture and stir just until no dry streaks remain. Transfer the batter to the prepared loaf pan.
4. Bake until golden brown on top and an instant-read thermometer inserted into the center of the loaf registers 200°F, 50 to 60 minutes. Let cool in the pan on a wire cooling rack for 30 minutes, then turn the bread out of the pan onto the rack and let cool completely.
5. While the cornbread cools, make the whipped honey butter: In a medium bowl with a handheld mixer, or in a stand mixer fitted with the paddle attachment, beat the butter on medium-high speed until creamy. Add the honey and continue beating until light and fluffy, 3 to 5 minutes, stopping to scrape down the sides of the bowl and the beaters or paddle with a rubber spatula as needed. On low speed, add the salt and cinnamon and beat until well mixed. Transfer to a small serving bowl. Slice the cornbread and serve with the whipped butter.

CANNED BREAD

CONTRIBUTED BY SQUIDWARD

The best thing since sliced can now be made in your very own kitchen thanks to Bikini Bottom's own (self-proclaimed) culinary genius, Squidward! "All it took was one look at my monthly grocery bill to realize it was time to figure out how to make this at home," he told us. "I nearly went mad trying to decide what spices to use, but I did it. I finally did it. Not that any of the Neanderthals in Bikini Bottom will appreciate it!"

MAKES 3 SMALL LOAVES

1¼ cups medium rye flour

½ cup fine yellow cornmeal

¾ teaspoon baking soda

½ teaspoon kosher salt

½ teaspoon ground allspice

¼ teaspoon ground cinnamon

½ cup raisins

½ cup unsulphured molasses

1¼ cups buttermilk

Salted butter and/or cream cheese, for serving

1 Wash and dry three empty 15-ounce aluminum food cans, making sure to remove the paper labels and any adhesive. Lay a small sheet of parchment paper on a work surface. Using one of the cans, trace three circles on the parchment. Then cut out each parchment circle along the inside of the line so the circles are a little smaller. Spray the inside of each can with nonstick cooking spray and line the bottom with a parchment circle. Set the cans aside.

2 Place a metal trivet large enough to hold the three cans on the bottom of a large stockpot. Add water to the pot to come about 3 inches above the top of the trivet. Place the pot on the stovetop and bring the water to a boil over medium heat while you prepare the bread batter.

3 In a medium bowl, whisk together the flour, cornmeal, baking soda, salt, allspice, and cinnamon, mixing well. Stir in the raisins. In a small bowl, stir together the molasses and buttermilk until smooth. Add the molasses mixture to the flour mixture and stir until combined.

4 Spray three small pieces of aluminum foil with nonstick cooking spray.

5 Divide the batter evenly among the three cans. The batter should fill each can about two-thirds full. Wrap the top of each can tightly with the prepared aluminum foil, then

CONTINUED

CANNED
BREAD
BEST THING
SINCE SLICED

CANNED BREAD

CONTINUED

stand the cans on the trivet. The water should come about halfway up the sides of the cans. Cover the pot and steam the breads until they are set to the touch and an instant-read thermometer inserted into the center of a loaf registers 190°F, 40 to 45 minutes.

6. Using oven mitts, carefully remove the cans from the pot (they'll be hot!) and transfer them to a wire cooling rack. Let cool, uncovered, for at least 30 minutes or up to 1 hour. Run a paring knife along the inside of one of the cans to loosen the bread sides and then tip the loaf out onto the rack. Repeat with the remaining two cans.
7. Slice the loaves and serve with butter and/or cream cheese. The loaves will keep in an airtight container at room temperature for up to 3 days.

RADIOACTIVE POPCORN

CONTRIBUTED BY BUBBLE BASS

All you die-hard Mermaid Man and Barnacle Boy fans can now have a taste of the glory that gave them their powers! According to Bubble Bass, who provided this recipe, absolutely *no* Mermaid Man and Barnacle Boy cosplay is complete without a batch of this sweet, salty treat, and anybody who says otherwise is a "fake fan."

***Historical Society Note*: This popcorn is *not* actually radioactive and will *not* grant you powers, super or otherwise, but it *will* satisfy your sweet tooth.**

MAKES 10 CUPS

10 to 12 cups air-popped popcorn

1 cup lightly packed light brown sugar

¼ cup honey

½ cup unsalted butter

1 teaspoon kosher salt

½ teaspoon baking soda

¼ teaspoon green gel food coloring

1. Preheat the oven to 200°F. Line a half sheet pan with parchment paper.
2. Put the popcorn into a very large heatproof bowl. Set aside.
3. In a large saucepan over medium heat, combine the sugar, honey, butter, and salt and cook, stirring constantly, until the butter melts, all the ingredients are evenly mixed, and the mixture comes to a boil. Stop stirring but continue cooking until the mixture forms a thick caramel sauce that registers 235°F on a candy thermometer.
4. Remove the pan from heat, add the baking soda and food coloring, and, using a long wooden spoon, stir vigorously until thoroughly incorporated. Work carefully, as the mixture will bubble up, rising considerably in the pan, and the sauce will be very hot. Keep stirring until the color is uniform, then pour it evenly all over the popcorn. Using a heat-resistant silicone spatula, fold the popcorn and caramel together until the popcorn is completely and evenly coated, then turn the popcorn out onto the prepared pan.
5. Spread the popcorn into an even layer on the pan and bake, stirring every 20 minutes or so, for about 1 hour. To test if the popcorn is ready, take a piece or two from the pan, let cool, and then sample. It should be dry and crunchy.
6. Let the popcorn cool completely on the pan on a wire rack, then break apart into smaller pieces to serve. The popcorn will keep in an airtight container at room temperature for up to 1 week.

DIABOLICALLY DELICIOUS DEVILED EGGS

CONTRIBUTED BY PLANKTON

We have to admit: Sometimes something surprisingly delicious comes from constant rejection. When we first reached out to Plankton, the diminutive and dastardly owner of The Chum Bucket, he "graciously" offered us the recipe to the "famous" Chum Burger. We said no, but thank you. He then offered us the recipe for Chum Fries. We said no. Then Chum Nuggets (no!), Chummy Joes (bleh), Chum-on-a-Stick (we're not even sure what that is). Finally, he shared with us his latest invention: Diabolically Delicious Deviled Eggs! Although we're pretty sure they're being used by Plankton to spy on us, the resulting recipe is oddly delicious and reminds us of a warm plate of cacio e pepe pasta.

SERVES 4 TO 6

12 eggs

¾ cup freshly grated pecorino romano cheese, plus more for garnish

⅓ cup mayonnaise

2 tablespoons olive oil

2 teaspoons freshly squeezed lemon juice

1 teaspoon Dijon mustard

¼ teaspoon kosher salt, plus more as needed

2 teaspoons freshly ground black pepper, plus more for garnish

1. Preheat the oven to 400°F. Line a half sheet pan with parchment paper.
2. Pour water to a depth of 1 inch into a large pot. Place a steamer basket or steamer insert in the pot. The water should come just up to but not touch the bottom of the basket or insert. Bring the water to a boil over high heat, then gently place the eggs in the steamer basket or insert. Cover the pot, turn down the heat to medium, and steam for 12 minutes.
3. While the eggs steam, prepare an ice bath. Place four cups of ice in a large bowl, then add enough water to the bowl to submerge the eggs completely.
4. When the eggs have finished steaming, immediately transfer them to the ice bath and let sit for 20 minutes. One at a time, remove the eggs from the ice bath, tap against a countertop, cracking the shell all over, and then peel away and discard the shell. As the eggs are peeled, transfer them to a clean medium bowl.
5. Using half of the cheese, make six 1-tablespoon-size mounds on the prepared sheet pan, spacing them well apart. Pat down each cheese mound into a flat circle. Bake until golden, 6 to 8 minutes. Let cool completely on the pan while you

CONTINUED

DIABOLICALLY DELICIOUS DEVILED EGGS

CONTINUED

finish preparing the eggs. (The cheese crisps can be made up to 1 day in advance. Store in an airtight container at room temperature.)

6 Halve each egg lengthwise. Using a small spoon, scoop out the yolk from each half into a medium bowl. Place the egg white halves, cut-side up, on a serving platter.

7 Add the mayonnaise, oil, lemon juice, mustard, salt, and pepper to the egg yolks and, using a handheld mixer, beat on medium speed until smooth. Using a rubber spatula, fold the remaining 6 tablespoons cheese into the yolk mixture, mixing well. Taste and adjust the seasoning with salt if needed.

8 Spoon the filling into the egg white halves, dividing it evenly. Or spoon the filling into a piping bag fitted with a medium star tip (or into a zip-top bag, seal the bag closed, and cut off a lower corner) and pipe the filling into the egg white halves. Garnish each filled egg half with a sprinkle each of pecorino romano and pepper. Cover the eggs and chill for at least 1 hour or up to 1 day.

9 When ready to serve, break each cheese crisp into four irregular wedges. Carefully insert one wedge into the filling of each egg half so it sticks up vertically.

CHICKEN CHORIZO NACHOS

CONTRIBUTED BY DIRTY BUBBLE

We were surprised Dirty Bubble came up with this recipe. When we asked what the inspiration behind this recipe was, he said nachos are basically a big, messy pile of stuff. And to that we have a correction. Nachos are a big, messy pile of *delicious* stuff. Could this mean a turning point for Dirty Bubble? Could he be turning . . . *good*? If his maniacal laughter is any indication, we have to assume not.

SERVES 4 TO 6

2 tablespoons neutral oil (such as canola or safflower oil)

12 ounces Mexican chorizo or plant-based chorizo alternative, preferably Soyrizo

2 breasts from a rotisserie chicken, boned, skinned, and shredded, or one 14-ounce can jackfruit, drained, rinsed, seeded, and shredded

One 14-ounce can diced roasted tomatoes, drained

½ teaspoon kosher salt, plus more as needed

1 pound tortilla chips, preferably freshly made

1 cup drained canned black beans, rinsed

½ small yellow onion, diced

½ cup shredded Cheddar Jack cheese

1. Preheat the oven to 400°F. Line a half sheet pan with parchment paper.
2. In a large skillet over medium-high heat, warm the oil. When the oil is shimmering, add the chorizo and cook, stirring and breaking it up with a wooden spoon, until cooked through and starting to crisp, 7 to 10 minutes.
3. Stir in the chicken and tomatoes, season with the salt, and cook, stirring frequently, until warmed through and the flavors are melded, about 5 minutes. Taste and adjust the seasoning with salt if needed.
4. Scatter the chips evenly over the prepared sheet pan. Scatter the chicken mixture evenly over the chips, followed by the beans, onion, and shredded cheese. Drizzle the cheese sauce over the top, then scatter the jalapeños evenly over the top.

CONTINUED

CHICKEN CHORIZO NACHOS

CONTINUED

½ cup Spicy Cheese Sauce (page 86) or store-bought queso dip

½ cup pickled jalapeño slices, homemade (page 89) or store-bought

¼ cup chopped fresh cilantro leaves

Sour cream, for serving

Volcano Sauce (page 84), for serving (optional)

Mild Bobby Sauce (page 87), for serving (optional)

5 Bake until the cheese is melted, 10 to 15 minutes. Let cool slightly, then scatter the cilantro over the top. Serve immediately with sour cream and with Volcano Sauce and Mild Bobby Sauce, if desired.

MR. KRABS'S MONEY BAGS

CONTRIBUTED BY MR. KRABS

We'd hoped Mr. Krabs, as one of Bikini Bottom's most popular business owners, might donate to our Historical Society, or maybe even pay for the printing costs of this book. He said he'd do us one better, called us "me boyos," and promised us bags and bags of the "green stuff." Our hopes soared at the idea of a cash donation . . . then we realized the green he was talking about was spinach. While you might not be able to pay the rent with these "money bags," you can at least fill your stomachs.

SERVES 4 TO 6

24 wonton wrappers

One 10-ounce bag frozen spinach, thawed

4 ounces cream cheese, at room temperature

¾ cup shredded mozzarella cheese

½ cup freshly grated Parmesan cheese

2 tablespoons crème fraîche

2 tablespoons mayonnaise

2 roasted garlic cloves (see Note, page 58)

Grated zest and juice of 1 lemon

½ teaspoon vinegar-based hot sauce, plus more as needed

One 14-ounce can artichoke hearts in water, drained and chopped

1. Preheat the oven to 350°F. Spray the cups of a 24-cup mini muffin tin with nonstick cooking spray. Place a wonton wrapper in each prepared cup, gently pressing it onto the bottom and up the sides. Lightly spray the wonton wrappers with cooking spray. Bake until just beginning to turn golden, 5 to 7 minutes. Transfer to a wire cooling rack and let cool slightly.
2. While the wonton wrappers are baking and cooling, prepare the filling. Put the spinach on the center of a clean kitchen towel, then gather up the sides of the towel and twist to create a bundle. Hold the bundle over the sink and continue twisting and squeezing until you've released as much of the moisture as possible. Transfer the spinach to a cutting board and chop finely.
3. In a large bowl, using a handheld mixer, beat the cream cheese on medium-high speed until smooth and creamy, 2 to 4 minutes. Add ½ cup of the mozzarella, the Parmesan, crème fraîche, mayonnaise, garlic, lemon zest and juice, and hot sauce and beat until well mixed. Stir in the spinach and artichoke hearts. Taste and adjust the seasoning with more hot sauce if needed.
4. Divide the filling evenly among the wonton wrappers (leaving them in the muffin tin). Sprinkle the tops with the remaining ¼ cup mozzarella, dividing it evenly. Bake until golden and the mozzarella is melted and gooey, 13 to 16 minutes. Let cool in the muffin tin on the wire cooling rack for 5 to 10 minutes before removing them from the tin (use a butter knife if needed to ease them out) and serving warm.

PINEAPPLE UNDER THE SEA-ZZA

CONTRIBUTED BY HAROLD AND MARGARET SQUAREPANTS

We believe there's no wrong way to enjoy a pizza—big, small, with pineapple, without pineapple. Live and let live and don't forget to vote for mayor, that's what we say. Harold and Margaret SquarePants came up with this cute little recipe. "Even back when he was just a baby sponge, our SpongeBob was obsessed with pineapple. He'd have it on everything, even these little pizzas. And now he *lives* in one. Can you believe it?" This is an easy recipe to scale up or down in case you find yourself cooking for just one or two people or for a big crowd.

SERVES 4

6 mini bagels

¾ cup pizza sauce

¾ cup shredded mozzarella cheese

¼ cup finely diced ham or plant-based ham alternative

2 tablespoons drained canned crushed pineapple

1. Preheat the oven to 450°F. Line a half sheet pan with parchment paper.
2. Split the bagels horizontally and place them, cut-side up, on the sheet pan. Spread 1 tablespoon of the sauce on each bagel half, then top with 1 tablespoon of the cheese. Sprinkle 1 teaspoon of the ham on top of the cheese, followed by ½ teaspoon of the pineapple.
3. Bake until the cheese is melted and starting to turn golden in spots, 12 to 15 minutes. Let cool for 5 to 10 minutes before serving.

CHAPTER TWO

ENTRÉES

ENTRÉES

We were thrilled with the variety of entrées the citizens of Bikini Bottom came up with for this book. There's Grandma's Mac and Cheese Pie (page 51), which is great on its own. (Has anybody else noticed the high turnover rate of Grandma's pet snails? Should we be concerned?) If you really wanna party 'til you're purple, try the pie topped with a scoop or two of Sandy's Texas-Style Chili con Carne (page 65). If you're looking for something a little more highbrow, might we point you to Squilliam's 5-Star Alfredo (page 56)? It goes deliciously with a glass of Fizzy Fang (page 157).

You'll also find fun, homey dishes in this chapter, like Karen's Holographic Meat Loaf (page 63), which we hear is Plankton's favorite, and Weiner Takes All (page 55), a Mexican street corn–inspired hot dog straight from the totally organic, definitely not robotic overlord mind of Weenie J. Wiener. There's a little something for everybody in these pages, unless you're purely a dessert person. If that describes you, what are you doing reading this chapter?! Skip the entrées and head straight over to page 91 for a cornucopia of sweet treats.

CHICKEN AND COCONUT RICE

CONTRIBUTED BY PATCHY THE PIRATE AND POTTY THE PARROT

Here's a simple one-pot meal for those busy days when you're tending your beloved pet snail, running a medium-size underwater city, or lifting weights at Mussel Beach and just don't have a lot of energy to make dinner. We got this recipe from Patchy the Pirate, who, as president of the SpongeBob SquarePants Fan Club, knows a thing or two about being busy. When we went to visit Patchy and asked him about his recipe, he waved us over and said, "Ahoy, there! Been cookin' up something fine in the galley, me and Potty have." Potty, Patchy's parrot, then swooped in and yelled, "Brawk! Speak for yourself!"

"Right you are, Potty! Can't manage a spatula with those wings, can ye? Well, fellow fanatics, this here's a fine and fragrant dish on its own, but for the spice-minded folk, we recommend a dash or two o' Tangy Sponge Sauce to make the flavors really sing, eh Potty?" Not unlike a politician, the parrot declined further comment.

SERVES 4

- Large pinch of saffron threads (about 40 to 50)
- 1 tablespoon boiling water
- 1 pound boneless, skinless chicken thighs, cut into 1-inch chunks or one 14-ounce can jackfruit, drained, rinsed, seeded, and cut
- 1 teaspoon kosher salt, plus more as needed
- ½ teaspoon freshly ground black pepper
- 1½ cups long-grain white rice (such as Carolina, basmati, or jasmine)
- One 14-ounce can coconut milk
- 1 cup low-sodium chicken or vegetable stock or broth
- 2 teaspoons peeled, grated fresh ginger
- 1 red bell pepper, seeded and cut into 1-inch pieces
- Chopped fresh cilantro, for garnish
- Lime wedges, for serving
- Tangy Sponge Sauce (page 88) or your favorite hot sauce, for serving (optional)

1. Crumble the saffron into a very small bowl. Add the boiling water and let sit to "bloom" the saffron as you prepare the other ingredients.
2. Season the chicken all over with the salt and pepper. Add the rice to a rice cooker, then add the coconut milk, stock, ginger, and saffron mixture and stir to mix well. Scatter the chicken and bell pepper evenly over the top. Cover the rice cooker and cook according to the manufacturer's instructions. (If you don't have a rice cooker, season the chicken as directed. Add the coconut milk, stock, ginger, and saffron mixture to a medium heavy saucepan, stir to mix, and bring to a boil over high heat. Stir in the rice, chicken, and bell pepper and return the mixture to a boil. Turn down the heat to a gentle simmer, cover, and cook until all the liquid has been absorbed, the chicken is cooked through, and the rice is tender, 15 to 18 minutes. Remove from the heat and let stand, covered, for 10 minutes before proceeding.)
3. Uncover and fluff and toss the rice and chicken with a rice paddle. Taste and adjust the seasoning with salt if needed.
4. Divide the rice and chicken among four bowls and garnish with cilantro. Serve with lime wedges and hot sauce, if desired.

MAC AND CHEESE PIE

CONTRIBUTED BY GRANDMA

Did you know that some snails really *love* mac and cheese? That's what Grandma tells us anyway. And what could be more grandma-like than turning mac and cheese into a delicious savory pie, complete with a cheese-cracker crust and spicy whipped cream for a little something extra? We also hear that this dish goes particularly well with a big scoop of Sandy's Texas-Style Chili con Carne (page 65) on top. "Nothing makes those snails more plump, juicy, and succulent than grandma's Mac and Cheese Pie," Grandma told us. "Yum yum!" We chose not to read too much into that. Enjoy!

SERVES 8

2½ cups crushed Cheez-It or other cheese crackers

4 tablespoons unsalted butter, melted and slightly cooled

1 egg white, lightly beaten

8 ounces sharp Cheddar cheese, shredded

1 tablespoon cornstarch

One 12-ounce can evaporated milk

2 teaspoons Dijon mustard

1 teaspoon hot sauce, plus more as needed

Kosher salt

2 cups elbow macaroni (8 ounces)

2 tablespoons freshly grated Parmesan cheese

1. Preheat the oven to 375°F.
2. To make the crust, in a medium bowl, combine 2 cups of the crushed crackers, the butter, and the egg white and stir until well blended and the mixture is the texture of wet sand. Transfer the mixture to a 9-inch deep-dish pie plate. Using your hands, spread the mixture evenly over the bottom and up the sides of the plate, then press firmly with the bottom of a measuring cup or water glass to compact well.
3. Bake the crust until darkened and set (it should look fairly dry), 12 to 15 minutes. Let cool in the pie plate on a wire cooling rack while you prepare the filling.
4. To make the filling, put the Cheddar into a medium saucepan. Sprinkle the cornstarch over the top, then toss to coat the cheese evenly with the cornstarch. Pour in the evaporated milk, place the pan over medium heat, and cook, stirring constantly, until the mixture is smooth and bubbly, about 10 minutes. Stir in the mustard and hot sauce and season with salt. Taste and adjust the seasoning with more salt and hot sauce if needed. Remove from the heat.

CONTINUED

MAC AND CHEESE PIE

CONTINUED

SPICY, SAVORY WHIPPED CREAM

½ cup heavy cream

1 teaspoon hot sauce

¼ teaspoon kosher salt

5 While the cheese sauce cooks, bring a large saucepan filled with salted water to a boil over high heat. Add the elbow macaroni, stir well, and cook until al dente, according to the package directions. Drain the macaroni, add to the cheese sauce, and stir until the macaroni is evenly coated with the sauce.

6 Add the macaroni to the cooled crust, smoothing it into an even layer. Top evenly with the remaining ½ cup crushed crackers and the Parmesan. Bake the pie until the top is golden, 15 to 20 minutes. Let cool on the wire cooling rack while you prepare the whipped cream.

7 To make the whipped cream: In a medium bowl, beat the cream with a handheld mixer on medium-high speed until thickened. Add the hot sauce and salt and continue beating until stiff peaks form.

8 Slice the warm pie and serve, topping each slice with a dollop of the whipped cream. Leftover pie will keep tightly covered in the fridge for up to 1 week.

SEA PEBBLE STEW

CONTRIBUTED BY FRED

Fred wanted to give us a few lines about this soup but couldn't make it to his interview—something about a leg injury? This is a good way to use up the last bits of dried beans you might have in the pantry. A mix is great for a variety of shapes, sizes, colors, and texture, but if you just have one or two types of bean, this stew will still be mighty tasty. This stew is very nourishing, so consider bringing it to cheer up any of your more accident-prone friends while they recover.

SERVES 4 TO 6

- 1 pound mixed dried beans (1 cup each pinto, kidney, and navy)
- 2 tablespoons olive oil
- 1 small yellow onion, diced
- 3 celery stalks, diced
- 3 medium carrots, peeled and diced
- 1 teaspoon kosher salt, plus more as needed
- ½ teaspoon freshly ground black pepper
- 4 garlic cloves, minced
- 8 cups low-sodium vegetable stock or broth or water
- 1 bay leaf
- 1 teaspoon dried thyme
- 8 ounces baby spinach, coarsely chopped
- Lemon wedges, for serving
- Mild Bobby Sauce (page 87), for serving
- Volcano Sauce (page 84), for serving

1. Rinse the beans under cold running water, then transfer to a large bowl and add water to cover by at least 3 inches. Let soak overnight. When ready to cook, drain the beans and set aside.
2. In a large Dutch oven over medium-high heat, warm the oil. When the oil is shimmering, add the onion, celery, and carrots and season with the salt and pepper. Cook, stirring occasionally, until the vegetables soften and the onion begins to turn translucent, 10 to 12 minutes. Add the garlic and cook, stirring constantly, until fragrant, about 30 seconds.
3. Add the beans, stock, bay leaf, and thyme, stir well, and bring to a boil. Turn down the heat to a simmer, cover, and cook, stirring occasionally, until the beans are tender and creamy inside, 1½ to 2 hours.
4. Uncover, scatter the spinach on top, re-cover, and remove the pot from the heat. Let sit for a few minutes to allow the spinach to wilt, then uncover and stir. Taste and adjust the seasoning with salt if needed. Serve with lemon wedges and hot sauce(s) of choice.

WIENER TAKES ALL

CONTRIBUTED BY WEENIE J. WIENER

After the snafu with the Weenie Bot calling us all weenies, we reached out directly to Weenie J. Wiener during the six- to eight-business-year waiting period to see if he might be willing to share a recipe with us (and possibly expedite that coupon we were promised). Shockingly, he provided us with this lovely recipe.

***Historical Society Note:* Mr. Wiener did attempt to turn us all into robots. Things didn't really end well. We're probably *never* going to get that coupon now. Sigh. At least this recipe will provide some comfort.**

SERVES 4

2 tablespoons olive oil

1 cup frozen fire-roasted corn

¼ teaspoon kosher salt

2 tablespoons mayonnaise

1 tablespoon Mexican crema

Grated zest and juice of 1 lime

1 teaspoon Tajín seasoning or chili powder

2 tablespoons finely chopped fresh cilantro leaves

2 tablespoons salted butter, at room temperature

4 split-top hot dog buns

4 meat or plant-based hot dogs

4 teaspoons crumbled Cotija cheese

Pickled jalapeños, homemade (page 89) or store-bought, for topping

1. In a medium skillet over medium heat, warm the oil. When the oil is shimmering, add the corn, season with the salt, and cook, stirring frequently, until warmed through, 3 to 5 minutes. Remove from heat and let cool.
2. In a medium bowl, stir together the mayonnaise, crema, lime zest and juice, and Tajín. Add the corn and stir and toss to coat evenly. Taste and adjust the seasoning with salt if needed, then stir in the cilantro.
3. Spread the butter on the cut sides of all four buns. Heat a large skillet over medium heat. When the pan is hot, place the buns, with one of the buttered sides down, in the skillet. Cook until golden, 3 to 5 minutes, then flip and cook until golden on the second side, 3 to 5 minutes longer. Transfer to individual plates, split-side up.
4. With the skillet over medium-high heat, add the hot dogs and sear, turning as needed to color evenly, until plumped and heated through, about 8 minutes total.
5. Divide the hot dogs evenly among the buns. Top each hot dog with one-fourth of the corn mixture, followed by 1 teaspoon of the cheese and a few jalapeño slices. Serve immediately.

5-STAR ALFREDO

CONTRIBUTED BY SQUILLIAM FANCYSON III

If you enjoy Alfredo sauce but wish it weren't so heavy, this butternut squash version from Squilliam is just the thing you need. In his own words:

The beauty and elegance of this dish is in its simplicity. I've traveled the world, performed with orchestras, lived in mansions—would I trade all of that for a bowl of this exquisitely creamy pasta?

No, of course not. I'm stinking rich. I can afford to do all of that, have my pasta, AND eat it too. The sauce carries the squash's natural sweetness, punctuated with pungent roasted garlic and salinated with salty aged cheese. It is truly a work of art, which should surprise no one. It is, after all, MY recipe. Now sally forth, humble chef. I wish you luck on your gustatory journey. Bon appétit!

SERVES 4 TO 6

5 cups peeled and 1-inch cubed butternut squash

1 teaspoon kosher salt, plus more as needed

½ cup freshly grated Parmesan cheese, plus more for serving

2 roasted garlic cloves (see Note)

Pinch of ground nutmeg

1 pound dried fettuccine

1. In a large pot, combine the squash with water to cover by about 2 inches. Bring to a boil over high heat, then turn down the heat to a strong simmer. Cook until a fork slides into a squash cube with little resistance, 8 to 12 minutes.
2. Meanwhile, fill a second large pot with salted water and bring to a boil over high heat.
3. When the squash is ready, scoop out the cubes with a wire skimmer or slotted spoon and transfer to a blender, reserving the cooking water in the pot. Add the salt, the Parmesan, garlic, nutmeg, and about 1 cup of the cooking liquid to the blender. Cover the blender with the lid slightly ajar (this is to allow steam to escape as you blend) and begin blending on low speed, gradually increasing the speed to high and continuing to blend until the sauce is smooth. Add more cooking water as needed to achieve a smooth, pourable consistency. Taste and adjust the seasoning with salt if needed, then cover tightly to keep warm.

CONTINUED

5-STAR ALFREDO

CONTINUED

4 Once the salted water comes to a boil, add the fettuccine, stir well, and cook until al dente, according to the package directions. Drain, transfer to a serving bowl, add the butternut squash sauce, and toss to coat evenly. Serve immediately, with Parmesan on the side.

NOTE Can't find roasted garlic at the store? No problem! To make your own, trim ½ inch or so off the top of a garlic head. Stand the head upright on a sheet of aluminum foil just large enough to enclose the head, drizzle the top with a teaspoon or two of olive oil, and then bring the sides of the foil up to make a tight packet. Place on a small sheet pan and roast in a preheated 375°F oven until the garlic cloves are tender and golden, 40 to 50 minutes. Remove from the oven, let cool, then unwrap and squeeze the cloves from their papery sheaths into a small airtight container. Cap tightly and store in the fridge for up to 1 week.

SWEDISH BARNACLE BALLS

CONTRIBUTED BY MR. KRABS

Before we were lucky to have these little meaty beauties in cans on every Barg'N-Mart shelf under the sea, Bikini Bottom's own Eugene Krabs learned how to make this dish while serving in the Navy. Known as Armor Abs Krabs to his Navy buddies, Mr. Krabs said the secret to his super strong physique is this protein-packed concoction, which becomes a cozy, flavorful meal when served over mashed potatoes and doused with lots of gravy.

SERVES 4

4 tablespoons neutral oil (such as canola or safflower)

1 large yellow onion, finely chopped

1¼ teaspoons kosher salt, plus more as needed

¼ cup almond flour

2 tablespoons whole milk

1 egg

1 pound 90 percent lean ground beef or plant-based ground meat alternative

½ teaspoon freshly ground black pepper

½ teaspoon ground allspice

½ teaspoon ground mustard

1 In a large skillet over medium-high heat, warm 2 tablespoons of the oil. When the oil is shimmering, add the onion, season with ¼ teaspoon of the salt, and cook, stirring occasionally, until translucent and beginning to brown at the edges, 10 to 12 minutes. Transfer to a small heatproof bowl and let cool. Set the pan aside.

2 Transfer half of the cooled onion to a large bowl, add the flour, milk, and egg, and beat until smooth. Add the beef and toss and stir to mix, breaking up the clumps into small pieces. Sprinkle evenly with the remaining 1 teaspoon salt, the pepper, allspice, ground mustard, ginger, nutmeg, and cloves. Stir first with a spoon and then knead gently with your hands to mix all the ingredients evenly.

3 Line a large sheet pan with parchment paper. Using a 1-tablespoon cookie scoop, scoop up some of the meat mixture and then release it onto the prepared pan. Repeat until all the meatballs are formed. If you don't have a cookie scoop, use a 1-tablespoon measure and roll each portion between your palms to form a ball, dampening your hands with water as needed to prevent sticking, before dropping it onto the prepared pan.

4 Return the skillet to medium-high heat and add the remaining 2 tablespoons oil. When the oil is shimmering, add half of the meatballs to the pan, spacing them evenly.

CONTINUED

SWEDISH BARNACLE BALLS

CONTINUED

- ¼ teaspoon ground ginger
- Pinch of ground nutmeg
- Pinch of ground cloves
- 1½ cups low-sodium chicken or vegetable stock or broth
- ½ cup heavy cream
- 1 teaspoon Dijon mustard
- 1½ tablespoons cornstarch mixed with 2 tablespoons cold water, for slurry
- Hot mashed potatoes, for serving
- Finely chopped fresh chives, for garnish

Cook, turning the balls with tongs as needed to sear evenly, until well browned and cooked through, 2 to 3 minutes on each side. Using the tongs, transfer to a large plate. Cook the remaining meatballs the same way and add them to the plate.

5 When all of the meatballs are cooked, return the remaining half of the cooled onion to the skillet over medium-high heat. Add the stock and, using a wooden spoon or spatula, stir and scrape the bottom of the skillet to loosen any browned bits. Stir in the cream and Dijon, then give the cornstarch mixture a quick stir to recombine and add it to the pan. Cook, stirring constantly, until the mixture has thickened and starts to bubble, about 5 to 7 minutes. Taste and adjust the seasoning with salt if needed. Return all of the meatballs to the skillet and stir and toss them in the gravy to coat evenly.

6 Spoon the meatballs and gravy over mashed potatoes. Garnish with chives and serve right away.

HOLOGRAPHIC MEAT LOAF

CONTRIBUTED BY KAREN

Is there anything more homey and comforting than meat loaf? Karen, Plankton's wife, provided us with this recipe, which she tells us is one of her husband's favorites. Perhaps it will become one of yours!

Nothing helps soften the sting of another day filled with failure like my homemade holographic meat loaf. Just ask my husband, Plankton! His days are always filled with failure, so I tend to make this one a lot. "What goes in it?" you ask. Hmm, after a quick analysis, I can tell you that this meat loaf is made up of meat and/or meat-like material 50 percent, loaf 50 percent. I hope that helps. Now, if you'll excuse me, I have to make a meat loaf of my own. I heard an explosion and cry of failure in the distance, so Plankton should be home any moment.

SERVES 4 TO 6

½ cup whole milk

2 eggs

2½ teaspoons Worcestershire sauce

2 slices white sandwich bread, torn into small pieces

2 tablespoons olive oil

1 small yellow onion, finely chopped

1 red bell pepper, seeded and finely diced

4 garlic cloves, finely chopped

1½ pounds meat loaf mix (see Note)

1 Preheat the oven to 375°F. Line a half sheet pan with parchment paper.

2 In a small bowl, whisk together the milk, eggs, and 1½ teaspoons of the Worcestershire sauce. Add the bread, toss to moisten evenly, and let soak while you complete the next step.

3 In a medium skillet over medium-high heat, warm the oil. When the oil is shimmering, add the onion and bell pepper and cook, stirring occasionally, until the onion is translucent and beginning to brown at the edges, 10 to 12 minutes. Add the garlic and cook, stirring constantly, until fragrant, about 30 seconds. Remove from the heat and transfer to a large heatproof bowl. Let cool for 10 minutes.

CONTINUED

HOLOGRAPHIC MEAT LOAF

CONTINUED

2 teaspoons kosher salt

½ teaspoon freshly ground black pepper

½ teaspoon dried thyme

½ teaspoon dried marjoram

½ cup ketchup

2 tablespoons maple syrup

1 teaspoon apple cider vinegar

¼ teaspoon chipotle chile powder

4 Break apart the meat loaf mix over the onion mixture, dropping it into the bowl as you work. Season with the salt, pepper, thyme, and marjoram. Add the soaked bread from step 2 and toss to mix everything together evenly. Shape into a loaf on the prepared sheet pan, gently compacting the mixture into a mound roughly 9 inches long and 5 inches wide.

5 In a small bowl, whisk together the ketchup, maple syrup, vinegar, chipotle chile powder, and the remaining 1 teaspoon Worcestershire sauce. Brush half of the sauce onto the surface of the meat loaf.

6 Bake the meat loaf, brushing more sauce on it every 15 minutes or so, until an instant-read thermometer inserted into the center of the loaf registers 165°F, 50 to 65 minutes.

7 Remove from the oven and let rest for 10 minutes before slicing and serving.

NOTE Use a prepared meat loaf blend from your butcher, prepare your own mix with any combination of ground beef and pork, or substitute a plant-based meat alternative.

SANDY'S TEXAS-STYLE CHILI CON CARNE

CONTRIBUTED BY SANDY CHEEKS

Another fine recipe from the ~~lab~~ kitchen of Sandy Cheeks! "Now, this one won't win you any world records for *spiciest* chili, but it might win one for *tastiest* chili," she tells us. While it's true this isn't the hottest chili you'll ever eat, we love how spice-forward it is, and you can always customize it yourself with more chipotle chile powder or even a little cayenne for that fire-breathing heat you crave.

SERVES 4 TO 6

4 tablespoons olive oil

1½ pounds meat loaf mix (see Note)

3 teaspoons kosher salt, plus more as needed

1 pound boneless pork ribs, cut into 1-inch chunks, or one 14-ounce can jackfruit, drained, rinsed, seeded, and cut into 1-inch chunks

2 large yellow onions, diced

6 garlic cloves, finely chopped

One 28-ounce can whole plum tomatoes, with juices

1 In a large Dutch oven over medium-high heat, warm 2 tablespoons of the oil. When the oil is shimmering, add the meat loaf mix, season with 1 teaspoon of the salt, and cook, stirring and breaking it up with a wooden spoon or spatula, until cooked through and well browned, 9 to 12 minutes. Using a slotted spoon, transfer the cooked meat to a medium bowl, leaving the fat in the pot.

2 If using the pork ribs, add them to the Dutch oven over medium-high heat, season with 1 teaspoon of the salt, and sear all over until well browned, about 3 minutes on each side. Using the slotted spoon, transfer the ribs to the bowl holding the meat loaf mix. If using jackfruit, skip this searing step and add the jackfruit to the bowl holding the plant-based meat.

CONTINUED

SANDY'S TEXAS-STYLE CHILI CON CARNE

CONTINUED

One 14-ounce can diced fire-roasted tomatoes, with juices

1 tablespoon ancho chile powder

1 tablespoon ground cumin

2 teaspoons sweet paprika

2 teaspoons smoked paprika

2 teaspoons ground coriander

1 teaspoon dried Mexican oregano or marjoram

½ teaspoon chipotle chile powder

½ teaspoon ground cinnamon

Pickled jalapeños, homemade (page 89) or store-bought, for serving

Spicy Cheese Sauce (page 86), for serving

Sour cream, for serving

Golden Loaf (page 27), for serving

3 Drain off all but 2 tablespoons of the fat from the Dutch oven, then add the onions and season with the remaining 1 teaspoon salt. Cook over medium-high heat, stirring occasionally, until translucent and beginning to brown at the edges, 10 to 12 minutes. As you cook the onions, scrape up any browned bits from the bottom of the pot. Splash in about ¼ cup water if needed to help loosen and scrape up the bits so they don't burn as you cook the onions. Add the garlic and cook, stirring constantly, until fragrant, about 30 seconds.

4 Add the cooked meat loaf mix and pork (or jackfruit) and the whole tomatoes with their juices and mash and stir until the tomatoes are broken apart. Add the diced tomatoes with their juices, ancho chile powder, cumin, both paprikas, coriander, oregano, chipotle chile powder, and cinnamon and stir well. Bring to a boil, then turn down the heat to a simmer and cook uncovered, stirring occasionally, until the pork is tender, about 2 hours.

5 Taste and adjust the seasoning with salt if needed. Serve the chili immediately with the the jalapeños, cheese sauce, sour cream, and golden loaf on the side.

NOTE Use a prepared meat loaf blend from your butcher, prepare your own mix with any combination of ground beef and pork, or substitute a plant-based meat alternative.

BIKINI BOTTOM

VOLCANO
SAUCE
HOT!

KING NEPTUNE'S SPEARS

CONTRIBUTED BY KING NEPTUNE

The Bikini Bottom Historical Society is thrilled and beyond grateful that King Neptune would share a royal recipe with us, and therefore *you*! This recipe has some significance to the royal family, as it appears King Neptune made this very dish for Queen Amphitrite when they were first courting. Not only do you get a piece of Bikini Bottom history here, but you get a piece of King Neptune and Queen Amphitrite's dating history too!

SERVES 4 TO 6

1 small yellow onion, coarsely chopped

2 garlic cloves

¼ cup freshly squeezed orange juice

¼ cup pineapple juice

2 tablespoons apple cider vinegar

1 tablespoon neutral oil (such as canola or safflower)

2 teaspoons kosher salt

½ teaspoon freshly ground black pepper

2 tablespoons ancho chile powder

1 tablespoon achiote paste

1 teaspoon ground cumin

1 teaspoon ground coriander

½ teaspoon dried Mexican oregano or marjoram

½ teaspoon dried thyme

1. In a blender, combine the onion, garlic, orange juice, pineapple juice, vinegar, oil, salt, pepper, ancho chile powder, achiote paste, cumin, coriander, oregano, thyme, chipotle chile powder, and cloves and blend until smooth.
2. Put the pork into a medium nonreactive bowl and pour in the marinade. Toss and stir to coat the pork evenly. Cover and refrigerate for at least 1 hour or up to 6 hours.
3. Prepare a charcoal or gas grill for direct-heat cooking over high heat. Alternatively, position an oven rack 4 to 6 inches from the heat source and preheat the broiler. Drain the pork, discarding the marinade, and gently pat the pork chunks dry with paper towels. Thread the pork and pineapple chunks onto metal skewers, alternating them as you go and starting and ending with pork. There should be more pork than pineapple on each skewer.
4. To grill the skewers, place them on the grill racks directly over the fire. To broil the skewers, arrange them on a half sheet pan and slide the pan under the broiler. Cook, turning as needed, until well seared with some charring here and there, about 2 minutes on each side. The cooking time may vary depending on the strength of your grill or broiler.

CONTINUED

KING NEPTUNE'S SPEARS

CONTINUED

- **½ teaspoon chipotle chile powder**
- **¼ teaspoon ground cloves**
- **1½ pounds boneless pork ribs or extra-firm tofu, cut into 1 by ½-inch chunks (see Note)**
- **1 pound fresh pineapple chunks (about 2 cups)**
- **Tangy Sponge Sauce (page 88), for serving**
- **Mild Bobby Sauce (page 87), for serving**
- **Volcano Sauce (page 84), for serving**
- **Warm flour or corn tortillas, for serving**

5 Serve the skewers immediately with hot sauce(s) of choice and warm tortillas.

NOTE If using tofu, drain well and pat dry with paper towels before cutting into chunks.

STIR-FRIED SPONGE BITS

CONTRIBUTED BY SPONGEBOB SQUAREPANTS

Our Vice President, Treasurer, Secretary, Under Secretary, Bursar, Registrar, Comptroller, and Chimney Sweep SpongeBob was inspired to share a piece of himself in this book. Literally. Maybe it's best if we let him tell you.

There I was, bits of sponge—me!—all tumbling down off of me and onto The Krusty Krab grill. I panicked! The only thing I could think of to do was to add some sauces and spices and, well, gobble the bits up.

Now, we don't recommend eating sponge, but we have a nice substitute that'll work just fine.

SERVES 4

One 14- to 16-ounce package extra-firm tofu

3 tablespoons neutral oil (such as canola or safflower)

1 cup broccoli florets

2 red bell peppers, seeded and cut into 1-inch pieces

4 green onions, white and light green parts, cut into 1-inch pieces

2 teaspoons peeled, grated fresh ginger

2 garlic cloves, minced

¼ teaspoon red pepper flakes

1. Line a sheet pan with parchment paper. Drain the tofu and pat dry with a paper towel, then cut into 1-inch cubes. Spread the tofu cubes in a single layer on the prepared sheet pan. Freeze the tofu for 6 hours, then transfer the pan to the fridge and thaw the tofu overnight. (This gives the tofu an extra-spongy texture, which allows it to absorb more of the sauce. You don't *have* to do this for the recipe to work, but the flavor and texture will be better if you do. You can also freeze the tofu, transfer it to an airtight container, and leave it in the freezer for a few months. Then when you are ready to make these sponge bits, move it to the fridge and let it thaw overnight.)
2. In a large wok over medium-high heat, warm 2 tablespoons of the neutral oil. When the oil is shimmering, add the broccoli and stir-fry until crisp and just starting to become tender, about 3 minutes.
3. Add the bell peppers and continue stir-frying until the peppers begin to soften, 2 to 3 minutes. Add the remaining 1 tablespoon neutral oil along with the green onions, ginger, garlic, and pepper flakes and stir-fry until fragrant, about 1 minute.

CONTINUED

STIR-FRIED SPONGE BITS

CONTINUED

3 tablespoons soy sauce

2 tablespoons mirin

1 tablespoon maple syrup

½ cup salted roasted cashews, chopped

1 tablespoon toasted sesame oil

Hot steamed white rice, for serving

4 Add the tofu, soy sauce, mirin, and maple syrup, give a quick stir, cover the wok, and cook for 2 minutes. Uncover and toss and stir to coat the tofu evenly with the sauce.

5 Remove from the heat, add the cashews, and drizzle with the sesame oil. Toss to mix and coat evenly, then serve immediately with bowls of hot steamed rice.

COCONUT GREEN BEANS

CONTRIBUTED BY THE FLYING DUTCHMAN

Devoted Historical Society member SpongeBob SquarePants volunteered to get this recipe from The Flying Dutchman. We were a little worried when he didn't come back until the next day. Spending the night on a glowing green ghost ship isn't the safest thing to do! But our brave yellow sponge returned in the morning with a tasty recipe for a delightful side dish and this note:

Yar har har har harrrr! Here's the recipe ya have requested. It's green and glorious, just like me! Had to return this here soul to ye, though. Couldn't take the nonstop yammering!

We thought it was weird that he wrote his laughter in the note too. We also thought it was weird that he thought we'd given him SpongeBob's soul.

SERVES 4

One 14-ounce package extra-firm tofu

1 teaspoon Japanese curry powder

2 tablespoons soy sauce

1 tablespoon mirin

8 ounces green beans, trimmed and cut into 2-inch lengths

½ cup unsweetened shredded dried coconut

2 tablespoons unrefined coconut oil

¼ cup sliced green onions, white and light green parts

2 garlic cloves, minced

2 teaspoons peeled, grated fresh ginger

½ cup salted roasted cashews

1. Drain the tofu, pat dry with a paper towel, and cut into 1-inch cubes. Transfer to a medium bowl, and add the curry powder, soy sauce, and mirin. Toss to coat evenly and let marinate while you prepare the other ingredients.
2. Bring a medium saucepan of salted water to a boil over high heat. Add the green beans and cook until bright green and tender-crisp, about 5 minutes. Drain and set aside.
3. Place a large wok over medium heat and add the shredded coconut. Cook, stirring and tossing constantly, until the coconut is fragrant and lightly toasted, 3 to 5 minutes. Transfer to a plate.
4. Return the wok to medium heat and add the oil. When the oil is shimmering, add the green onions, garlic, and ginger and cook, stirring constantly, until fragrant, about 1 minute. Add the tofu along with the marinade and the green beans and cook, stirring and tossing constantly, until the tofu is warmed through, 3 to 4 minutes.
5. Return the toasted coconut to the wok and cook, tossing and stirring constantly, until evenly distributed, about 1 minute. Remove from the heat and stir in the cashews. Serve hot.

PATRICK STAR PASTINA

CONTRIBUTED BY PATRICK STAR

We honestly weren't sure what to expect from Patrick when we asked for a recipe but were pleasantly surprised by this soup inspired by sopa de fideos. It's a tasty little tomato soup, gently spiced, with toasty diminutive star-shaped pasta floating throughout. We found it not only comforting but also surprisingly complex given that it calls for just a handful of ingredients. When we asked Patrick what he liked most about the dish, he said, "Heh heh heh, it's like a big pot of tiny little me's!"

SERVES 4

½ cup neutral oil (such as canola or safflower)

½ medium white onion, diced

½ teaspoon kosher salt

½ teaspoon freshly ground black pepper

2 garlic cloves, minced

¼ teaspoon ground cumin

One 14½-ounce can whole plum tomatoes, with juices

8 ounces star-shaped pastina (stelline)

4 cups low-sodium chicken or vegetable stock or broth

1. In a medium saucepan over medium-high heat, warm 1 tablespoon of the oil. When the oil is shimmering, add the onion, season with the salt and pepper, and cook, stirring occasionally, until the onion begins to turn translucent, 7 to 10 minutes. Add the garlic and cumin and cook, stirring constantly, until fragrant, about 30 seconds. Remove from the heat.
2. In a blender, combine the onion mixture and the tomatoes and their juices and blend until smooth. Set aside.
3. Wipe out the saucepan, place over medium heat, and add the remaining oil. When the oil is shimmering, add the pastina and cook, stirring constantly, until toasted to a light golden brown, 7 to 10 minutes.
4. Add the broth and tomato mixture to the pastina, increase the heat to medium-high, and bring to a boil. Cook, stirring occasionally, until the pastina is tender, about 5 minutes or according to the package directions.
5. Remove from the heat and spoon into individual bowls. Serve hot.

THE KRABBY PATTY

CONTRIBUTED BY THE KRUSTY KRAB

We know. We can't believe it either. After coaxing, begging, bargaining, and nearly resorting to stealing, we finally got SpongeBob to convince Mr. Krabs to reveal the secret recipe to the Krabby Patty. We just know that this one recipe will make the whole book worth the price you paid and then some. Think of it as a very small contribution to pay for a massive part of Bikini Bottom's history! With that, we turn things over to SpongeBob:

The history of the Krabby Patty goes way, wayyyy back to when my wonderful boss, Mr. Krabs, was just a little kid. When you look at one, you might just see bun, patty, lettuce, cheese, onion, tomato, ketchup, mustard, pickles, bun. But there's more, so much more, to a Krabby Patty. There's a . . . come here . . . shhhh . . . secret formula that only Mr. Krabs knows. For as long as I can remember, anytime I think about the secret formula, all I can recall are these words: 'The Krabby Patty formula is the sole property of The Krusty Krab and is only to be discussed in part or in whole with its creator, Mr. Krabs. Duplication of this formula is punishable by law. Restrictions apply, results may vary.' That's it until now.

Now that we've gotten the legalese out of the way, I, SpongeBob SquarePants, esteemed member of the Bikini Bottom Historical Society am proud to say that the recipe to the Krabby Patty is . . .

CONTINUED

RECIPE
FOR A
KRABBY
PATTY

THE
KRUSTY
KRAB
ENTER

WHAT IN THE SALTY SEVEN SEAS IS THIS?

THE KRABBY PATTY

CONTINUED

MAKES [redacted]

1 [redacted]

2 [redacted]

3 [redacted]

4 [redacted]

5 [redacted]

6 [redacted]

CONTINUED

NEVER IN A MILLION YEARS, YE SCALAWAGS!

—MR. KRABS

VOLCANO SAUCE

If you're the type who loves a hot hot sauce, this is the hottest hot sauce in all of Bikini Bottom. Our most enthusiastic member of the Historical Society, SpongeBob, provides a kitchen-friendly version of the epic concoction, and warned us that even a single drop may be too powerful for non-heat-seekers. We recommend a couple drops over some Chicken Chorizo Nachos (page 37) to temper its awesome, volcanic power.

MAKES ABOUT 2 CUPS

- 1 medium carrot, peeled and coarsely chopped
- 1 large shallot, quartered
- 8 large habanero chiles, stemmed
- 2 tablespoons olive oil
- 1 teaspoon kosher salt, plus more as needed
- 6 roasted garlic cloves (see Note, page 58)
- 1 cup apple cider vinegar
- 1 teaspoon sugar

1. Preheat the oven to 425°F. Line a half sheet pan with parchment paper.
2. Put the carrot, shallot, and chiles in a medium bowl, drizzle with the oil, and then toss to coat evenly. Season with the salt and toss again to mix well.
3. Turn the vegetables out onto the prepared sheet pan, spreading them in a single layer. Roast until tender and starting to char in some spots, 20 to 25 minutes.
4. Transfer the roasted vegetables to a blender and add the garlic, vinegar, and sugar. Cover the blender with the lid slightly ajar (this is to allow steam to escape as you blend) and begin blending on low speed, gradually increasing the speed to high and continuing to blend until the sauce is smooth. Taste and adjust the seasoning with salt if needed.
5. Let cool to room temperature, then transfer to a sterilized airtight glass bottle or jar. The sauce will keep in the fridge for up to 2 weeks.

CONTINUED

Clockwise from top left: **Volcano Sauce, Mild Bobby Sauce, Tangy Sponge Sauce, and Spicy Cheese Sauce.**

SPICY CHEESE SAUCE

It might surprise you that one of the secret ingredients for this spicy cheese sauce is . . . spicy cheese. As Karen would say, "50 percent spicy cheese, 50 percent sauce." But this sauce gets an extra kick or two of heat from hot sauce *and* pickled jalapeños. Use it to make your Krabby Patty extra spicy, add it to your nachos, drizzle it on chili, or just use it as a dip for chips!

MAKES ABOUT 1½ CUPS

8 ounces pepper Jack cheese

1 tablespoon cornstarch

One 12-ounce can evaporated milk

1 tablespoon Mild Bobby Sauce (opposite page), Volcano Sauce (page 84), or store-bought hot sauce

2 to 4 tablespoons finely minced pickled jalapeños, homemade (page 89) or store-bought

1. Shred the cheese on the largest holes of a box grater. Transfer to a medium saucepan, add the cornstarch, and toss to mix well.
2. Pour in the evaporated milk, then place the pan over medium-low heat and cook, stirring constantly, until smooth, 7 to 10 minutes.
3. Stir in the hot sauce and pickled jalapeños, remove from the heat, and serve immediately. Leftover sauce will keep in an airtight container in the fridge for up to 5 days. To reheat, warm gently in a small saucepan over low heat, adding a splash of evaporated milk if needed to thin to a good consistency.

MILD BOBBY SAUCE

Unlike the Volcano Sauce (page 84), and as the name suggests, this is a milder hot sauce for the not so daring, brought to you by Mr. Krabs. It's mild on heat but strong on flavor—great for adding to chili con carne (page 65), nachos (page 37), or anything that needs a tiny bit of heat and a little extra flavor.

MAKES ABOUT 2 CUPS

1 pound red Fresno or jalapeño chiles, stemmed and seeded

4 garlic cloves

1 small yellow onion, coarsely chopped

2 teaspoons kosher salt

1 cup apple cider vinegar

1 In a food processor or high-speed blender, combine the chiles, garlic, onion, salt, and vinegar and pulse a few times to mix. Then run the food processor or blender on high speed until the sauce is smooth.

2 For a very smooth sauce, strain through a fine-mesh sieve into a large measuring cup with a spout before transferring it to a sterilized airtight glass bottle or jar. The hot sauce will keep in the fridge for up to 2 weeks.

CONTINUED

THE KRABBY PATTY

CONTINUED

TANGY SPONGE SAUCE

Another saucy hit from Mr. Krabs (isn't he just brilliant?), the secret to this sauce's tanginess is a big hit of pineapple chunks and pineapple juice. Like the Mild Bobby Sauce (page 87), this one is relatively low on heat but big on flavor. We love it on some freshly grilled King Neptune's Spears (page 70) or dashed onto bowls of Chicken and Coconut Rice (page 48).

MAKES ABOUT 2 CUPS

1 cup fresh pineapple chunks

2 red Fresno or jalapeño chiles, stemmed

1 small carrot, peeled and coarsely chopped

1 small yellow onion, coarsely chopped

2 garlic cloves

1 teaspoon kosher salt

¼ cup pineapple juice

½ cup apple cider vinegar

1. In a food processor or high-speed blender, combine the pineapple chunks, chiles, carrot, onion, garlic, salt, pineapple juice, and vinegar and pulse a few times to mix. Then run the food processor or blender on high speed until the sauce is smooth.
2. For a very smooth sauce, strain through a fine-mesh sieve into a large measuring cup with a spout before transferring it to a sterilized airtight glass bottle or jar. The hot sauce will keep in the fridge for up to 2 weeks.

PICKLED JALAPEÑOS

Everything needs a secret ingredient, even secret ingredient ingredients! These tangy jalapeños are the key to SpongeBob's Spicy Cheese Sauce (page 86) and Dirty Bubble's Chicken Chorizo Nachos (page 37) and go great on Sandy's Texas-Style Chili Con Carne (page 65). But what is it that makes them so special? Just ask SpongeBob: "Aw, there are lots of things in these spicy little fellas that make them extra tasty. Spices, vinegar, garlic! But what makes them taste extra special and super good is *love*!"

MAKES ABOUT 1 QUART

2 cups water

1 cup apple cider vinegar

1 tablespoon sugar

2 teaspoons kosher salt

2 bay leaves

2 whole cloves

1 teaspoon coriander seeds

8 black peppercorns

¼ teaspoon allspice berries

8 large green jalapeño chiles, cut into ¼-inch-thick coins

6 garlic cloves

4 sprigs cilantro

1. In a medium saucepan, combine the water, vinegar, sugar, salt, bay leaves, cloves, coriander, peppercorns, and allspice and bring to a boil over high heat. Add the jalapeños and garlic and return to a boil. Turn down the heat to a simmer and cook, stirring occasionally, until the jalapeños have turned a pale green but are still tender-crisp, about 10 minutes.
2. Remove the pan from the heat and stir in the cilantro. Let cool to room temperature, then transfer to a sterilized 1-quart mason jar, cap tightly, and refrigerate for 48 hours before serving. The jalapeños will keep in the fridge for up to 1 month.

CHAPTER THREE

DESSERTS

DESSERTS

Finally, desserts—the chapter some (or maybe all?) of you have been waiting for. To research this part of the book, we sent SpongeBob door-to-door to ask Bikini Bottomites how they feel about desserts. The responses ranged from "I love sheet cake!" to "Bikini Bottom has a historical society?" to "Tell your pink friend to get his head out of my cookie jar!"

This chapter has desserts that should satisfy just about every flavor of sweet tooth. If you're into . . . chocolate . . . (phew). If you're into *that*, there are a bunch of options, including Grandma SquarePants's Icebox Cake (page 95), which mixes *that* with peanut butter, a classic combo. But there's also a Double Dark Deep Sea Cake (page 111), which is layers and layers of . . . *that*. Then there are Sandy's Texas Sheet Cake (page 102) and Plankton's Chum Bucket Cookies (page 114). Options abound if you're into chocolate!

If you're more into fruity desserts, there are SpongeBob's Mini Pineapple Upside-Down Cakes (page 127), which are great for serving a crowd; SpongeGar's Grilled Pineapple with Coconut Whipped Cream (page 97), which is a lighter option; and Hedvig Fishtrap's Kerglooginpfiefer mit Schlusinberry Klabber Sauz (page 129), which is . . . really something!

If, like Sandy Cheeks, you're more into something with a nutty crunch, you can turn to Sandy's Land Nut Pie (page 123), Frank's Seanut Brittle (page 107), and Sand Tarts (page 121), which we are led to believe don't actually contain sand. We know, we couldn't believe it either. False advertising, if you ask us. We'd have pressed the issue, but that recipe came from the Nematodes, and it just didn't seem worth the trouble.

Whatever your taste may be when it comes to desserts, we just know you'll find something that'll make you finish your meal on a strong (and sweet) note. And if you don't find something you like, well . . . at least you can go to bed knowing that you helped make *our* dreams come true, even if we fell short of making *your* sweet dreams come true.

ICEBOX CAKE

CONTRIBUTED BY GRANDMA SQUAREPANTS

This peanut butter and chocolate icebox cake is a breeze to make and comes from the kitchen of longtime Bikini Bottom resident Grandma SquarePants. She loves how simple this cake is, and it's one of her number-one specialties (apart from her cookies and coral quiche with seaweed butter, of course). "Icebox cakes have been popular since I was a little sponge and they're just *lovely* to make on a hot day because you don't need to fire up the oven."

SERVES 8 TO 10

One 15-ounce container whole-milk ricotta cheese

1 cup creamy peanut butter (not natural; see Note)

4 tablespoons confectioners' sugar

2 teaspoons vanilla extract

¼ teaspoon almond extract

1½ cups cold heavy cream

One 10- to 12-ounce package thin chocolate sandwich cookies (such as Oreo Thins)

½ cup salted peanuts, finely chopped

1 Line a 9 by 5-inch loaf pan with plastic wrap, allowing it to overhang all four sides by about 3 inches.

2 In a food processor, combine the ricotta and peanut butter and pulse just until barely mixed. There should still be some streaks of peanut butter showing. Add 3 tablespoons of the sugar and the vanilla and almond extracts and process, stopping two or three times to scrape down the sides of the bowl, until the mixture is very smooth, 2 to 4 minutes.

3 In a large bowl, combine the cream and the remaining 1 tablespoon sugar. Using a handheld mixer, beat on medium-high speed until soft peaks form, 2 to 4 minutes. The timing will depend on the power of your mixer.

4 Add the peanut butter–ricotta mixture to the whipped cream and, using a rubber spatula, gently fold together the two mixtures until smooth and homogenous.

5 Add a scoop of the peanut butter mixture to the bottom of the prepared loaf pan and smooth it into an even layer about ½ inch thick. Arrange a single layer of cookies on top (you should be able to fit about eight cookies). Top the cookie layer with another ½-inch-thick layer of the peanut butter mixture, and follow with another layer of

CONTINUED

ICEBOX CAKE

CONTINUED

cookies. Repeat the layers until you have used up all of the peanut butter mixture, ending with a layer of the peanut butter mixture.

6 Give the pan a couple of short, sharp taps on a countertop to knock out any air bubbles. Bring the overhanging plastic wrap up and over the peanut butter mixture, covering completely and sealing tightly. Place the pan in the freezer for at least 4 hours or up to 1 month.

7 When ready to serve, pull the plastic wrap away from the top of the peanut butter mixture and invert a serving platter on top of the pan. Grasp the pan and platter together and flip them in one smooth movement. Lift off the pan and then peel off the plastic wrap. Press the peanuts evenly over the outside of the cake. Use a serrated knife to slice the cake. Store any leftover cake well wrapped in plastic wrap in the fridge for up to 3 days.

NOTE Natural peanut butter separates easily, which can negatively impact the texture of this dessert.

GRILLED PINEAPPLE WITH COCONUT WHIPPED CREAM

CONTRIBUTED BY SPONGEGAR

We, at the Bikini Bottom Historical Society, deeply value firsthand knowledge, which is why we used Mermaid Man and Barnacle Boy's time machine to travel to the prehistoric era to meet with SpongeBob's ancestor SpongeGar. We managed to get this primitive recipe out of him, and it's surprisingly good since all he seems to do is hold things over "fwee fwee," er, fire. SpongeGar had this to say about his grilled pineapple recipe: "Fwee fwee make food good. No use fwee fwee for cream though. But still good." And right he is! Fire *does* make pineapple good—the sugars get caramelized and the flavor becomes more complex—and the coconut whipped cream is a lovely addition.

SERVES 4 TO 6

COCONUT WHIPPED CREAM

One 14-ounce can full-fat coconut milk, refrigerated overnight and unshaken

1 tablespoon confectioners' sugar

Pinch of kosher salt

1 teaspoon vanilla extract

½ teaspoon coconut extract

1. To make the coconut whipped cream: Open the can of chilled coconut milk. With a small spoon, scoop out the firm layer of coconut fat solidified on top into a medium bowl, being careful to leave the separated coconut water in the can. You can use the coconut water for a smoothie or drink it as is.
2. Using a handheld mixer, beat the coconut fat on medium-high speed until soft peaks form, 3 to 6 minutes. Add the confectioners' sugar, salt, and vanilla and coconut extracts and continue to beat just until fully incorporated. Cover and chill until serving.
3. To make the grilled pineapple: In a small bowl, whisk together the brown sugar, cinnamon, salt, ginger, allspice, and nutmeg. Set aside.
4. Oil the grates of a charcoal or gas grill, then prepare a fire for direct-heat cooking over high heat. While the grill heats, using a large knife, trim off the top and bottom of the pineapple. Stand the pineapple upright on a cutting board and slice off the skin, cutting downward in long

CONTINUED

GRILLED PINEAPPLE WITH COCONUT WHIPPED CREAM

CONTINUED

GRILLED PINEAPPLE

2 tablespoons dark brown sugar

1 teaspoon ground cinnamon

½ teaspoon kosher salt

½ teaspoon ground ginger

¼ teaspoon ground allspice

Pinch of ground nutmeg

One 4- to 5-pound pineapple

strips and following the curve of the pineapple. Using the tip of a small knife, cut out the "eyes." Using the large knife, cut the pineapple lengthwise into eight wedges, then trim off the tough core from each wedge. Cut the wedges in half crosswise. You should have sixteen wedges each 3 to 4 inches long.

5 Place the pineapple wedges on a serving tray and sprinkle them all over with the brown sugar mixture, coating them evenly. Place the pineapple wedges on the grill grates directly over the fire and grill, turning once, until lightly charred on both sides and slightly softened, 2 to 3 minutes on each side. As the wedges are ready, return them to the serving tray.

6 Serve the pineapple wedges warm with the chilled whipped cream.

COCO-HUT SALAD

CONTRIBUTED BY DOODLEBOB

This was a tricky recipe to nail down because it comes from the warped mind of DoodleBob. Of course, he didn't have a recipe handy, so we just set him loose in a kitchen and observed his, er, artistry at work. We watched as he threw ingredient after ingredient into a bowl, spinning around like a little chaos gremlin. We, perhaps against our better judgment, tried it, and . . . it's good! It's a very sweet, coconut-forward dessert with a little tang from pineapple and lime and crunch from toasty pecans. As DoodleBob would describe it, "Herblabba flibbidy bloomblobba! Gribbity von babba!" Couldn't have said it better ourselves, DoodleBob!

SERVES 6

- One 8-ounce can crushed pineapple in juice, undrained
- Grated zest and juice of 1 lime, plus more grated zest for topping
- One 3.4-ounce package instant coconut-flavored pudding mix
- 1½ cups mini marshmallows
- ¾ cup pecan halves, toasted and chopped
- One 8- or 9-ounce container coconut-based whipped topping
- 6 maraschino cherries

1. In a large bowl, stir together the crushed pineapple and its juice, lime zest and juice, and pudding mix. Add the marshmallows and ½ cup of the pecans and toss to mix well.
2. Using a rubber spatula, fold the whipped topping into the pineapple mixture until well blended. Cover and chill until set, at least 1 hour or up to 5 days.
3. Divide among six small dessert bowls. Sprinkle with the remaining ¼ cup pecans, dividing them evenly, and a little lime zest. Top each bowl with a maraschino cherry and serve chilled.

SANDY'S TEXAS SHEET CAKE

CONTRIBUTED BY SANDY CHEEKS

Sandy Cheeks brings more of her native Texas flavor to Bikini Bottom with this scrumptious chocolate cake. "I take a particular liking to this cake, it's super-duper chocolaty and gets a big ol' sprinkling of yummy, dummy nuts! Smack my tail and call me twitchy, I think I need to make another of these right quick!"

And off she goes! This cake is great for a crowd because it makes a lot, but if you're throwing a history-makin' party, you can double all of the ingredients and make it in a half sheet pan to serve a crowd of twenty-five or more.

MAKES ONE 9 BY 13-INCH CAKE; SERVES 12 TO 16

CAKE

½ cup unsalted butter

½ cup hot brewed coffee

¼ cup natural cocoa powder

½ teaspoon kosher salt

1 cup all-purpose flour

¾ cup granulated sugar

½ teaspoon baking soda

⅓ cup Mexican crema or crème fraîche, or ¼ cup sour cream plus 1 to 2 tablespoons whole milk

1 egg

2 teaspoons vanilla extract

1. To make the cake: Preheat the oven to 350°F. Generously butter a quarter sheet pan.
2. In a small saucepan over medium heat, melt the butter, stirring or swirling the pan occasionally. When the butter is fully melted, stir in the hot coffee, cocoa powder, and salt, then bring to a boil and cook, stirring occasionally, until smooth, 2 to 3 minutes. Remove the pan from the heat.
3. In a large bowl, whisk together the flour, granulated sugar, and baking soda. In a small bowl, whisk together the crema, egg, and vanilla until smooth.
4. Scrape the cocoa mixture into the flour mixture. (Save the saucepan to reuse for making the frosting later. You won't even need to rinse it.) Stir the cocoa and flour mixtures together until smooth. It will have the consistency of a thick paste, almost like cookie dough. Stir in the crema mixture until smooth.

CONTINUED

SANDY'S TEXAS SHEET CAKE

CONTINUED

FROSTING

6 tablespoons unsalted butter

¼ cup natural cocoa powder

¼ teaspoon kosher salt

2 to 4 tablespoons whole milk

2 teaspoons vanilla extract

1¼ cups confectioners' sugar

¾ cup chopped toasted pecans

5 Pour the batter into the prepared pan, smoothing it into an even layer with an offset spatula. Bake until a toothpick inserted into the center of the cake comes out mostly clean with a few moist crumbs clinging to it, 15 to 18 minutes. Let cool in the pan on a wire cooling rack.

6 While the cake cools, make the frosting: Return the saucepan to medium heat and melt the butter, stirring or swirling the pan occasionally. When the butter is fully melted, stir in the cocoa, salt, and 2 tablespoons of the milk until smooth. Then stir in the vanilla and confectioners' sugar and remove the pan from heat. Continue to stir until smooth, glossy, and thick but pourable. If the mixture is too thick, add up to 2 tablespoons more milk to reach the desired consistency.

7 Pour the frosting evenly over the warm cake and, using an offset spatula, spread into a smooth, even layer. Sprinkle the pecans evenly over the top, then gently press them into the frosting to ensure they stick. Let the cake cool to room temperature before serving. Leftover cake will keep tightly covered at room temperature for up to 3 days.

SPONGE CANDY

CONTRIBUTED BY THE ANCHOVIES

The Anchovies gave us this tasty, crunchy candy in honor of SpongeBob, their favorite fry cook at their most beloved restaurant. We don't speak Anchovy, but for those who do, here's what they had to say: "Meep-meep-meep-meep-meep-meep-meep-meep-meep-meep-meep-meep-meep-meep-meep-meep-meep-meep-meep-meep-meep-meep-meep-meep-meep-meep-meep-meep-meep-meep-meep-meep-meep-meep-meep-meep-meep-meep-meep-meep-meep-meep-meep-meep-meep-meep-meep-meep-meep-meep-meep-meep-meep-meep-meep-meep-meep-meep-meep-meep-meep-meep-meep-meep-meep-meep."

One thing we do know is that you have to get the sugar *very* hot, so, kids, make sure you have an adult helping you with this recipe.

MAKES ABOUT 1 POUND

1 cup sugar

1 cup dark corn syrup

1 tablespoon distilled white vinegar

1 tablespoon baking soda (see Note)

NOTE Make sure there are no lumps in your baking soda. Mash with the back of a spoon or press through a fine-mesh sieve before starting the recipe.

1. Line a 9 by 13-inch baking pan with parchment paper, allowing it to overhang all four sides by about 2 inches. Spray the parchment with a light coating of nonstick cooking spray or grease with a very thin layer of butter.
2. In a deep medium-large heavy pot (or Dutch oven), combine the sugar, corn syrup, and vinegar. Place over medium heat and cook, undisturbed, until the sugar melts, about 5 minutes. Once the sugar has melted, continue cooking, swirling the pot occasionally, until the mixture registers 300°F on a candy thermometer.
3. Remove the pan from the heat, add the baking soda, and, using a long wooden spoon, stir vigorously until thoroughly incorporated. Work carefully, as the mixture will bubble up, rising considerably in the pot. Pour into the prepared baking pan and let cool to room temperature.
4. Lift the candy out of the pan using the overhanging parchment. Transfer to a cutting board or clean work surface and break the candy apart into irregular chunks. Transfer to an airtight container and store at room temperature. The candy will stay fresh for up to 1 week.

SEANUT BRITTLE

CONTRIBUTED BY FRANK AND THE PALACE OF PRANKS

Sweet, salty, crunchy—there's nothing pranky about this recipe from Frank, the owner of the Palace of Pranks. Frank also tells us that Virginia peanuts are the best to use for the brittle because they're big and extra crunchy, but any salted peanuts will do. Just be careful not to put the brittle in a can and get it all mixed up with the fake cans of Seanut Brittle, or you might fall for one of Frank's many pranks (speaking from experience).

You have to get the sugar *very* hot, so, kids, make sure you have an adult helping you with this recipe.

MAKES ABOUT 1 POUND

1 cup sugar

6 tablespoons unsalted butter

⅓ cup honey

1 teaspoon vanilla paste

⅓ cup water

¾ teaspoon baking soda (see Note, page 105)

¼ teaspoon kosher salt

1¼ cups salted Virginia peanuts

1. Butter a half sheet pan.
2. In a deep medium saucepan, combine the sugar, butter, honey, vanilla paste, and water. Place over medium-low heat and cook, undisturbed, for 5 minutes. Once the sugar has dissolved, continue cooking, swirling the pan occasionally, until the mixture registers 300°F on a candy thermometer.
3. Remove the pan from the heat, add the baking soda and salt, and, using a long wooden spoon, stir vigorously until thoroughly incorporated. Work carefully, as the mixture will bubble up, rising considerably in the pan. Using a heat-resistant silicone spatula, immediately fold in the peanuts, distributing them evenly, then pour the mixture onto the prepared sheet pan. Using the silicone spatula, spread the mixture into a thin, even layer. Let cool to room temperature, about 1 hour.
4. Break apart the peanut brittle into irregular chunks. Transfer to an airtight container and store at room temperature. The brittle will stay fresh for about 1 month.

KRAKATOA MAGMA CAKES

CONTRIBUTED BY CAPTAIN MAGMA

From the International Justice League of Super Acquaintances' hottest member, Captain Magma, these *magma* cakes are rich, chocolaty, and full of molten red caramel "magma." Just one cut into a cake and you'll make history and release the delicious fury of Krakatoa. Captain Magma has a quick serving suggestion for you: "Don't forget to yell my signature catchphrase—KRAKATOA!—when you cut into your cake and release the magma caramel."

MAKES 4 INDIVIDUAL CAKES

CARAMEL FILLING

¼ cup dulce de leche, at room temperature

1 tablespoon unsalted butter, at room temperature

¼ teaspoon red or orange gel food coloring

Pinch of kosher salt

LAVA CAKES

½ cup unsalted butter, cut into small pieces

6 ounces semisweet to bittersweet chocolate (50 to 75 percent cacao), finely chopped

2 eggs

2 egg yolks

⅓ cup lightly packed dark brown sugar

¼ teaspoon kosher salt

1 teaspoon vanilla extract

2 tablespoons all-purpose flour

1. To make the caramel filling: Line a small sheet pan with parchment paper. In a small microwave-safe bowl, stir together the dulce de leche, butter, food coloring, and salt until smooth. If the ingredients are not mixing well, microwave on low power in 5-second bursts, stirring well after each burst until smooth. Divide the filling into four equal mounds on the prepared sheet pan, spacing them well apart. Freeze until very firm, at least 1 hour or up to overnight.
2. Preheat the oven to 450°F. Grease four 6-ounce ramekins with butter, then dust lightly with flour, tapping out the excess. Place the ramekins on a half sheet pan.
3. To make the lava cakes: Pour water to a depth of about 1 inch into a medium saucepan. Rest a heatproof bowl in the rim of the pan, making sure the bottom of the bowl isn't touching the water. Bring the water to a boil over medium-high heat, then turn down the heat to a simmer. Add the butter and chocolate to the bowl and heat, stirring constantly, until melted and smooth. Remove from the heat and set aside.
4. In a large bowl, using a handheld mixer, beat together the eggs, egg yolks, brown sugar, and salt on low speed, gradually increasing to high speed until pale, thickened, and almost doubled in volume, 3 to 5 minutes. The mixture is ready when it leaves trails of thick ribbons behind it that slowly melt away as you move the beaters through it. Beat in the vanilla extract.

CONTINUED

KRAKATOA MAGMA CAKES

CONTINUED

5 Stir the chocolate mixture into the egg mixture until smooth, then fold in the flour just until no white streaks remain. Divide the batter evenly among the four prepared ramekins. Remove the filling mounds from the freezer and place a mound in the center of each cake. Press on each mound to immerse it a bit more than halfway into the batter. Do not submerge it.

6 Bake the cakes until the tops look completely set but feel soft when gently pressed, 10 to 14 minutes. Let the cakes cool on the pan on a wire cooling rack for 2 minutes, then invert a small serving plate or bowl over each ramekin. Using potholders to protect your hands, grasp a ramekin and plate together and flip them in one smooth, quick movement. Repeat with the remaining ramekins. Let sit until you hear the gentle thud of each cake falling out of its ramekin. Lift off the ramekins and serve immediately.

DOUBLE DARK DEEP SEA CAKE

CONTRIBUTED BY TOM

Hoo boy, this was an . . . *interesting* one to get. This recipe comes from Tom, and we had to give it this name instead of simply calling it what it is: a chocol—whoops, sorry, we shouldn't have used the C-word. We named this not just to avoid sending Tom into a spiral, but because it uses black cocoa (wait, we can use cocoa but not ch— . . . never mind), which gives it a unique flavor and makes it resemble the deepest, darkest depths of the sea.

SERVES 8 TO 12

CAKE

2½ cups all-purpose flour

2 teaspoons baking powder

1 teaspoon baking soda

1 teaspoon kosher salt

1 cup hot brewed coffee

1 cup black cocoa powder

½ cup unsalted butter, cubed

½ cup neutral oil (such as canola or safflower)

3 eggs, at room temperature

1 cup granulated sugar

1 cup lightly packed dark brown sugar

½ cup buttermilk, at room temperature

1 tablespoon vanilla extract

1. To make the cake: Preheat the oven to 350°F. Butter two 9-inch round cake pans. Line the bottom of each pan with a parchment paper circle, then dust the sides of the pans with black cocoa powder, tapping out the excess.
2. In a small bowl, whisk together the flour, baking powder, baking soda, and salt.
3. In a small saucepan over medium-low heat, stir together the coffee and cocoa powder until smooth. Add the butter and continue stirring until the butter melts and the mixture is smooth. Stir in the oil, mixing well, and remove from the heat.
4. In a large bowl, using a handheld mixer, beat together the eggs and the granulated and brown sugars on medium-high speed until pale, thickened, and almost doubled in volume, 3 to 5 minutes. The mixture is ready when it leaves trails of thick ribbons behind it that slowly melt away as you move the beaters through it. Beat in the buttermilk and vanilla extract just until well mixed.
5. Add the coffee-cocoa mixture to the egg mixture and beat on medium speed until fully incorporated, stopping the mixer and scraping down the sides and along the bottom of the bowl as needed. Turn the mixer off and add the flour

CONTINUED

DOUBLE DARK DEEP SEA CAKE

CONTINUED

FROSTING

4 cups confectioners' sugar

1 cup black cocoa powder

¼ teaspoon kosher salt

¾ cup unsalted butter, at room temperature

½ cup heavy cream

2 teaspoons vanilla extract

mixture. On low speed, mix just until no dry streaks of flour remain. Scrape down the sides of the bowl again, stirring and folding the batter to ensure it's homogenous.

6 Divide the batter evenly between the prepared pans. Bake until a toothpick inserted into the center of each cake layer comes out mostly clean with a few moist crumbs clinging to it, 22 to 28 minutes. Let cool in the pans on a wire cooling rack for 30 minutes, then turn out onto the wire rack, peel off the parchment, turn upright, and let cool completely.

7 To make the frosting: In a medium bowl, sift together the confectioners' sugar, cocoa powder, and salt. In a large bowl, using the handheld mixer, beat the butter on high speed until smooth and creamy. Add the confectioners' sugar mixture, cream, and vanilla and mix on low speed until moistened. Gradually increasing the mixer speed to high, beat until the mixture is smooth, fluffy, and thick, 4 to 6 minutes.

8 Using a serrated knife, trim the domed top off of each cake layer (these make a nice little baker's treat while you work). Place one of the cakes on a platter or cake stand. Scoop about 1 cup of the frosting on top of the layer and, using an offset spatula, spread the frosting evenly and smoothly over the top of the layer, stopping just short of the edge. Place the second cake layer, trimmed-side down, on top of the frosting, gently pressing it into the frosting.

9 Scoop half of the remaining frosting on top of the cake and spread it evenly, then use the remaining frosting to cover the sides, smoothing the frosting with the offset spatula. If you have any remaining frosting, dollop it on the top of the cake and use the back of a large soup spoon or serving spoon to create decorative swoops.

10 Slice and serve the cake. Leftover cake can be covered with a cake dome and stored at room temperature for up to 3 days or in the fridge for up to 1 week. If refrigerating the cake, for the best texture, cut the slices and allow them to come to room temperature before serving.

CHUM BUCKET COOKIES

CONTRIBUTED BY PLANKTON

These chocolaty cookies come from Plankton, and their origin is pretty on brand. "I originally made these to trick that *fool* Mr. Krabs. They're gold on the outside, which should have gotten that money-loving nincompoop distracted enough to let me steal the Krabby Patty formula. Inside, though, they're surprisingly complex, just like my heart!! The plan was, and I quote my wife, 'an utter failure.' But at least they taste good." The gold sugar on the outside gives them a pleasing crunch and pretty gold sparkle, but you can swap it out for raw sugar (such as turbinado or demerara) if you prefer.

MAKES 24 COOKIES

1½ cups all-purpose flour

⅓ cup black cocoa powder

½ cup unsalted butter, at room temperature

½ cup granulated sugar

½ teaspoon kosher salt

1 tablespoon vanilla extract

Few drops of almond extract

1 egg

½ cup gold sanding sugar

1. In a small bowl, whisk together the flour and cocoa powder. Set aside.
2. In a large bowl, using a handheld mixer (or in a stand mixer fitted with the paddle attachment), beat together the butter, granulated sugar, and salt on medium-high speed until light and fluffy, 3 to 5 minutes, stopping the mixer and scraping down the sides of the bowl two or three times as needed. Add the vanilla, almond extract, and egg and continue to beat on medium-high speed until well mixed.
3. Turn off the mixer and add the flour mixture. On low speed, mix just until no dry streaks of flour remain in the dough.
4. Turn the dough out onto a clean work surface. Using your palms, roll the dough into a log about 2 inches in diameter and 6½ inches long. Wrap the log in plastic wrap and refrigerate for at least 1 hour or up to 3 days.
5. About 15 minutes before you are ready to bake, preheat the oven to 350°F. Line two half sheet pans with parchment paper.

CONTINUED

CHUM BUCKET COOKIES

CONTINUED

6 Spread the sanding sugar in a shallow medium dish. Unwrap the dough log and roll it in the sanding sugar, coating it evenly and pressing gently to ensure the sugar sticks. Transfer the log to a cutting board and, using a very sharp knife, trim off about ¼ inch from each end to remove any uneven sections. Then cut the log into twenty-four ¼-inch-thick slices. Lay the slices on the prepared sheet pans, spacing them evenly. Place one pan in the freezer while you bake the other pan.

7 Bake the cookies until set and dry looking, 15 to 17 minutes. Let cool on the pan on a wire cooling rack, then transfer the cookies to the rack to cool completely. Bake and cool the second pan of cookies the same way. The cookies will keep in an airtight container at room temperature for up to 1 week.

TRIPLE GOOBERBERRY SUNRISE

CONTRIBUTED BY GOOFY GOOBER'S ICE CREAM PARTY BOAT

The estate of Reginald Goober, the late, great owner of Goofy Goober's Ice Cream Party Boat and longtime benefactor to the Bikini Bottom Historical Society, was kind enough to share its recipe for the Triple Gooberberry Sunrise. This signature sundae of GGICPB will not only bring a smile to your face because it's so delicious and sweet, but it'll smile right back at you! It's big enough to share, but we'll totally understand if you don't want to. The secret to this sundae is the homemade fudge sauce, which you can make up to a week in advance. You'll have more fudge sauce than you need for one sundae, so be sure to save the leftovers (or eat them with a spoon).

SERVES 3

FUDGE SAUCE

- ¼ cup lightly packed dark brown sugar
- 2 tablespoons Dutch-processed cocoa powder
- ¼ teaspoon kosher salt
- 3 ounces semisweet to bittersweet chocolate (50 to 75 percent cacao), finely chopped
- ¼ cup dark corn syrup
- ¼ cup heavy cream
- 1 tablespoon unsalted butter
- 2 teaspoons vanilla extract

1. To make the fudge sauce: In a small saucepan, whisk together the brown sugar, cocoa powder, and salt until no lumps remain. Add the chocolate, corn syrup, cream, and butter, place over medium-low, and heat, stirring constantly, until well mixed.
2. Increase the heat to medium and continue stirring until the mixture comes to a boil. Cook, stirring constantly, until thickened, glossy, and smooth, 3 to 5 minutes longer. Remove from the heat, stir in the vanilla, and let cool to room temperature. The fudge sauce can be made up to 1 week in advance. Store in an airtight container in the fridge, then bring to room temperature before assembling.
3. To assemble the sundae: Line a sheet pan with parchment paper. Peel the bananas and cut in half crosswise. Eat one of the banana halves or reserve for another use. Place a toothpick halfway into the tip of each banana half. Skewer the three cherries onto the toothpicks, making sure two cherries are horizontal on the halves with two picks, for the arms, and one cherry is vertical on the half with one pick, for the top of the head. Place the banana halves on the sheet pan and freeze for 30 minutes.

CONTINUED

TRIPLE GOOBERBERRY SUNRISE

CONTINUED

TO ASSEMBLE

2 barely ripe medium bananas

3 maraschino cherries with stems, patted dry

3 cups vanilla ice cream

1 blue candy-coated chocolate

1 green candy-coated chocolate

1 red candy-coated chocolate

One 1½-inch piece red licorice rope

4 Create three 1-cup-size scoops of the ice cream and mound them on top of one another in a small freezer-safe ice-cream bowl. The first scoop should just about fill the bowl, with the remaining scoops standing above the rim of the bowl. Make two small divots (about the size of the candies) in the top scoop. These will be where the eyes will go. Make a third divot in the top scoop in between and slightly below the eyes. This will be for the nose. Freeze the ice cream, bowl and all, for 1 hour.

5 Working quickly, spread 3 to 4 tablespoons of the fudge sauce on the top scoop of ice cream. Place the blue candy in the left-eye divot, the green candy in the right-eye divot, and the red candy in the nose divot. Use the licorice rope to create a smile. Stick the banana half with the vertical cherry in the top of the sundae. Place the two "arm" banana halves on either side of the sundae so they rest on the bowl. Serve immediately with three spoons (or one if you prefer to enjoy your sundae solo).

SAND TARTS

CONTRIBUTED BY NEMATODES

Everyone in Bikini Bottom knows that Nematodes can be . . . shhh . . . *a menace*. But did you know that they're also exceptional bakers? It's true! Contrary to their name, Sand Tarts don't actually contain any sand, but they do get a little dusting—a *sanding*, if you will—of cinnamon sugar on top that gives them a sandy appearance! They're also *very* addictive, which explains why the Nematodes like them so much. They're thin, buttery, and sweet, and each one gets a nice pop of extra nutty flavor from a toasted pecan on top.

MAKES 36 COOKIES

1¾ cups all-purpose flour

¼ cup cornstarch

½ cup sugar

½ teaspoon kosher salt

½ cup cold unsalted butter, cut into ½-inch cubes

1 egg yolk

2 to 4 tablespoons heavy cream

2 teaspoons vanilla extract

TOPPING

1 egg white

¼ cup sugar

2 teaspoons ground cinnamon

Pinch of ground nutmeg

36 pecan halves, toasted

1. To make the cookie dough, in a food processor, combine the flour, cornstarch, sugar, and salt and process briefly to mix. Scatter the butter cubes on top and pulse until the mixture resembles wet sand and no big pieces of butter remain.
2. In a small bowl, whisk together the egg yolk, 2 tablespoons of the cream, and the vanilla. Pour this mixture into the food processor and pulse until a smooth dough forms. If the mixture seems too dry, add 1 tablespoon of the cream at a time and pulse again until smooth.
3. Turn the dough out onto a clean work surface and, using your palms, shape into a log about 2 inches in diameter, flattening the ends as best you can. The log should be about 5 inches long. Wrap tightly in plastic wrap and place in the freezer until very firm but not frozen solid, 30 to 60 minutes.
4. While the dough chills, preheat the oven to 350°F. Line three half sheet pans with parchment paper.
5. Unwrap the dough log and place on a cutting board. Using a very sharp knife, trim off about ¼ inch from each end to remove any uneven sections. Then, cut the log into thirty-six cookies. They should be no thicker than ⅛ inch thick and, ideally, thinner. Divide the cookies evenly among the sheet pans, spacing them evenly apart. If the dough tears, just press the tear together with a finger. It's okay if they look a little irregular. Place two of the sheet pans in the fridge while you work on the first pan.

CONTINUED

SAND TARTS

CONTINUED

6 To make the topping: In a small bowl, lightly beat the egg white until loosened. In a separate small bowl, whisk together the sugar, cinnamon, and nutmeg.

7 Brush a very thin layer of the egg white on the top of each cookie. (Don't be tempted to work on and bake more than one sheet pan at a time. You don't want the egg white to soak into the cookies.) Sprinkle a small amount of the sugar mixture on top of each cookie, then place a single pecan half in the center, gently pressing it into the surface.

8 Bake the cookies until the edges begin to brown and the centers look dry and set, 12 to 15 minutes. Let cool on the pan on a wire cooling rack for 5 minutes, then transfer the cookies to the rack to cool completely. Repeat with the remaining two sheet pans of cookies, topping them and baking them one at a time. The cookies will keep in an airtight container at room temperature for up to 1 week.

LAND NUT PIE

CONTRIBUTED BY SANDY CHEEKS

We've been blessed with not just one but *two* dessert recipes from resident scientist, explorer, and inventor Sandy Cheeks! In her own words:

Nothing says home to me like pecan pie. Of course, home isn't about barbecues or pecan pies. Home is where you're surrounded by critters that care about ya. I just so happen to enjoy showing critters I care about 'em by invitin' 'em over for barbecues and pecan pies!

Sandy's trick to an excellent pecan pie is to use maple syrup, which goes beautifully with toasted pecans. A little bit of almond extract adds another layer of nutty flavor, which Sandy *says* is optional but does make a difference.

SERVES 8 TO 12

CRUST

1½ cups all-purpose flour, plus more as needed

1 tablespoon granulated sugar

¾ teaspoon kosher salt

½ cup cold unsalted butter, cut into ½-inch cubes

3 tablespoons ice-cold water

1. To make the crust: In a food processor, combine the flour, granulated sugar, and salt and process briefly to mix. Scatter the butter cubes on top and pulse until the mixture resembles wet sand with some pea-size butter pieces visible. Transfer the mixture to a medium bowl, add the water, and stir until a shaggy dough forms. Using your hands, and working quickly, mix until a smooth dough forms. Then shape the dough into a thick disk, wrap in plastic wrap, and chill for 1 hour. Toward the end of the chilling time, preheat the oven to 400°F.
2. Lightly flour a work surface, then unwrap the dough disk and place on the floured surface. Working from the center toward the edges, roll out the dough into a circle about 12 inches in diameter. Carefully roll the dough circle around the rolling pin, position the pin over a 9-inch pie plate, unroll the dough, and center it in the pie plate. Gently press the dough into the bottom and up the sides. Use a paring knife to trim away the excess dough, leaving a ¾-inch overhang. Fold the overhang over itself to create an edge and then crimp as you like, either pinching

CONTINUED

LAND NUT PIE

CONTINUED

FILLING

3 cups pecan halves, toasted

3 eggs

½ cup maple syrup

½ cup light corn syrup

⅓ cup lightly packed dark brown sugar

½ teaspoon ground cinnamon

¼ teaspoon ground nutmeg

½ teaspoon kosher salt

6 tablespoons unsalted butter, melted and cooled

1 tablespoon vanilla extract

¼ teaspoon almond extract (optional)

the dough with your index finger and thumb to create a wavy look or gently pressing with the tines of a fork for a more rustic look. Line the dough with aluminum foil and fill with pie weights, uncooked rice or dried beans, or granulated sugar.

3 Bake the crust for 15 minutes, then remove the weights and foil (if you used sugar, let it cool and transfer to a storage container to be used for a future recipe). Prick the bottom of the crust all over with a fork, then return the crust to the oven and bake until the bottom looks dry, 10 to 15 minutes longer. Let the pie crust cool completely on a wire cooling rack. Lower the oven temperature to 375°F.

4 To make the filling: Finely chop 2 cups of the pecan halves and transfer to a small bowl. Reserve the remaining 1 cup pecans.

5 In a large bowl, whisk the eggs until frothy. Add the maple syrup, corn syrup, brown sugar, cinnamon, nutmeg, and salt and whisk until smooth. While whisking constantly, add the butter in a slow, steady stream, mixing well. Whisk in the vanilla and almond extract (if using). Fold in the chopped pecans.

6 Pour the egg mixture into the cooled pie crust, allowing it to spread into an even layer. Arrange the reserved 1 cup whole pecan halves in concentric circles on the top of the filling.

7 Bake the pie for 40 minutes, then tent with foil, covering the whole pie (this will keep the crust and nuts from burning). Continue to bake until the pie is just barely set and still jiggles slightly in the very center, 15 to 20 minutes longer. Let cool to room temperature on a wire cooling rack.

8 Slice and serve. Leftover pie will keep tightly covered in the fridge for up to 1 week.

MINI PINEAPPLE UPSIDE-DOWN CAKES

CONTRIBUTED BY SPONGEBOB SQUAREPANTS

A beautiful cake recipe from SpongeBob inspired by his home, the only pineapple under the sea. Anybody who knows SpongeBob knows he loves to celebrate, and these cakes are perfect for any gathering.

These are so much fun to make because they look like boring old yellow cakes until you flip them out of the pan, and then, bam! Surprise! Caramel, pineapple, and a yummy cherry! These little cakes are the perfect party food . . . oh, that reminds me. We should have a party right now!

MAKES 12 INDIVIDUAL CAKES

TOPPING

6 tablespoons unsalted butter

⅔ cup lightly packed dark brown sugar

1 teaspoon ground cinnamon

½ teaspoon ground ginger

1 teaspoon vanilla extract

12 canned pineapple slices in juice, juices reserved and patted dry

12 maraschino cherries, stemmed and patted dry

1 Preheat the oven to 350°F. Spray two 6-cup jumbo muffin tins with nonstick cooking spray.

2 To make the topping: In a small saucepan over medium heat, combine the butter and brown sugar and heat, stirring occasionally, until the butter has melted and the sugar has dissolved. Remove from heat, then stir in the cinnamon, ginger, and vanilla extract until the mixture is smooth. Divide the mixture evenly among the prepared muffin cups. Add a pineapple slice to each muffin cup, then place a cherry in the center of each pineapple slice.

3 To make the cakes: In a medium bowl, whisk together the flour, baking powder, baking soda, and salt. Set aside.

4 In a stand mixer fitted with the paddle attachment (or in a large bowl with a handheld mixer), mix together the sugar, eggs, and egg yolk on low speed until the sugar is evenly moistened, about 2 minutes. Increase the speed to medium and beat until lightened and thick, 3 to 4 minutes. Then increase the speed to high and beat until the mixture has thickened and nearly doubled in volume, 3 to 5 minutes.

CONTINUED

MINI PINEAPPLE UPSIDE-DOWN CAKES

CONTINUED

CAKES

2 cups all-purpose flour

1½ teaspoons baking powder

½ teaspoon baking soda

1 teaspoon kosher salt

1½ cups granulated sugar

3 eggs, at room temperature

1 egg yolk, at room temperature

⅓ cup buttermilk, at room temperature

⅓ cup pineapple juice (from the canned pineapple), at room temperature

⅓ cup neutral oil (such as canola or safflower)

4 tablespoons unsalted butter, melted and cooled

1 tablespoon vanilla extract

5 Decrease the mixer speed to low, add the flour mixture, and mix just until no white streaks remain. Turn off the mixer and add the buttermilk, pineapple juice, oil, butter, and vanilla extract, then mix on medium-high speed until smooth, 2 to 3 minutes. Turn off the mixer and, using a rubber spatula, scrape the beaters and scrape down the sides and along the bottom of the bowl, then fold the batter a few times to make sure all the ingredients are well mixed.

6 Divide the batter evenly among the muffin cups, adding about ½ cup batter to each cup. Bake the cakes until a toothpick inserted into the center of one of the cakes comes out mostly clean with a few moist crumbs clinging to it, 20 to 25 minutes. Let the cakes cool in the muffin tins on a wire cooling rack for 30 minutes.

7 Working with one muffin tin at a time, run a thin knife around the inside edge of each muffin well to loosen the cake sides, then invert a sheet pan or platter over the muffin tin. Grasp the pan and muffin tin together and flip them in one smooth movement. Allow the cakes to fall out, giving the muffin tin a few sharp taps with a wooden spoon if they don't fall out on their own, then lift off the tin. Repeat with the second muffin tin. Transfer the cakes to small dessert plates and serve warm. The cakes are also great at room temperature. Leftover cakes will keep in an airtight container in the fridge for up to 3 days.

KERGLOOGINPFIEFER MIT SCHLUSINBERRY KLABBER SAUZ

CONTRIBUTED BY "HEDVIG FISHTRAP"

This, erm, *colorful* dessert is a classic German dish made by real, actual, verified German person Hedvig Fishtrap (we're pretty sure it's actually Squidward, but please just play along). We're not really sure what this is, but Hedvig had this to say: "Oh ya, mein kiddievinks love der kerglooginpfiefer! It makes them sing mit joy!" From what we can tell from tasting it, it seems to be a pile of crispy meringue cookie bits, sweet-and-sour strawberry rhubarb compote, and zesty lime whipped cream.

SERVES 6 TO 8

MERINGUES

2 egg whites

¼ teaspoon kosher salt

¼ teaspoon cream of tartar

⅔ cup granulated sugar

¼ teaspoon blue gel food coloring

1 Preheat the oven to 200°F. Line a half sheet pan with parchment paper. Fit a large piping bag with a large star tip.

2 To make the meringues: In a stand mixer fitted with the whisk attachment, beat the egg whites on medium-low speed until frothy. Add the salt and cream of tartar, increase the speed to medium, and continue beating, adding the granulated sugar 1 tablespoon at a time and waiting for about 1 minute before adding the next tablespoon. When all of the sugar has been added, increase the speed to medium-high and beat until the mixture is glossy and holds firm peaks, 3 to 5 minutes. Add the food coloring and beat on high speed until incorporated, about 1 minute longer.

3 Scoop the meringue into the piping bag and twist the top closed. Pipe the meringue onto the prepared sheet pan, making each mound about 2 inches wide and 1½ inches tall and spacing them about ¾ inch apart. You should have about 48 meringue cookies (see Notes).

CONTINUED

KERGLOOGINPFIEFER MIT SCHLUSINBERRY KLABBER SAUZ

CONTINUED

STRAWBERRY RHUBARB COMPOTE

8 ounces rhubarb stalks, trimmed and diced

¼ cup freshly squeezed orange juice

1 quart strawberries (about 1½ pounds or 5 cups), hulled and quartered

½ cup granulated sugar

1 tablespoon freshly squeezed lemon juice

1 teaspoon ground cinnamon

Pinch of kosher salt

4 Bake the meringues for 2 hours, then turn off the oven. Let cool in the oven with the oven door closed for 30 minutes, then prop the oven door open with a wooden spoon and let cool for 1 hour longer. Remove the pan from the oven, gently peel the meringues off the parchment, and set them aside in an airtight container at room temperature until needed.

5 While the meringues bake and cool, make the compote: In a medium saucepan combine the rhubarb and orange juice and bring to a boil over medium-high heat. Turn down the heat to medium and cook, stirring occasionally, until the rhubarb softens and begins to break down, 3 to 6 minutes.

6 Stir in the strawberries, granulated sugar, lemon juice, cinnamon, and salt and continue cooking, stirring occasionally, until the strawberries soften and the mixture turns red from the strawberry juice, 10 to 12 minutes. Remove from the heat, let cool for 15 minutes, and then transfer to an airtight container and chill for at least 3 hours. You can make the compote up to 5 days in advance. Just keep it in the fridge in an airtight container until ready to serve.

CONTINUED

KERGLOOGINPFIEFER MIT SCHLUSINBERRY KLABBER SAUZ

CONTINUED

LIME WHIPPED CREAM

2 cups heavy cream

2 tablespoons confectioners' sugar

¼ teaspoon kosher salt

1 tablespoon grated lime zest

1 teaspoon freshly squeezed lime juice

¼ teaspoon electric green gel food coloring

2 cups fresh strawberries, hulled and quartered, for topping

7 To make the whipped cream: Wash and dry the mixer bowl and whisk attachment (or use a large bowl and a handheld mixer). Add the cream, confectioners' sugar, salt, and lime zest to the bowl and beat on low speed until mixed, then gradually increase the speed to medium-high, beating until soft peaks form. Add the lime juice and food coloring and beat until blended.

8 Now, assemble the dessert! You can serve it in a large parfait dish or in six to eight individual dessert cups. However you do it, the process is the same. First, crumble 3 to 4 cookies per person being served. Then begin with a layer of compote, followed by a layer of crumbled meringues, and then a layer of whipped cream. Repeat until the dish or cups are nearly full, ending with a layer of whipped cream and reserving some of the cream for topping. Spoon the quartered berries on top and finish with a dollop of the whipped cream. Serve immediately.

NOTES This makes more meringues than you'll need for the recipe. Store the extras in an airtight container at room temperature for up to 1 week.

If you'd like to save time and don't care about the color of your meringue cookies, store-bought meringue cookies are fine to use here!

MRS. PUFF'S CREAM PUFFS

CONTRIBUTED BY MRS. PUFF

These cream puffs aren't just *made* by Mrs. Puff. They kinda look like her too! They're a little bit Mrs. Puff and a little bit SpongeBob, who we've been told by some of his classmates is her favorite student of all time. "I got the inspiration for the filling when SpongeBob showed up for picture day just *covered* in peanut butter. That boy . . . he's no chocolate cake, that's for sure. The only driving he's good at is driving me crazy!" The filling for these cream puffs is tasty enough to eat on its own. We like to serve it like pudding, topped with some chocolate shavings or crunchy chocolate pearls.

MAKES 12 CREAM PUFFS

PEANUT BUTTER PASTRY CREAM

- 2 cups whole milk
- 1 vanilla bean, split lengthwise
- 3 tablespoons cornstarch
- ¼ teaspoon kosher salt
- ½ cup sugar
- 4 egg yolks
- ⅓ cup creamy peanut butter (not natural)
- 2 teaspoons vanilla extract

1. To make the pastry cream: Pour the milk into a medium saucepan. Using a paring knife, carefully split the vanilla bean lengthwise. Using the tip of the knife, scrape the seeds from inside each pod half, then add the seeds and pod halves to the milk. Place the pan over medium heat and warm the milk until just barely simmering. Then remove the pan from the heat, cover, and let sit for 30 minutes. Uncover and remove the vanilla pod.
2. While the vanilla bean steeps in the milk, in a medium bowl, whisk together the cornstarch, salt, and sugar until no lumps remain in the cornstarch. Add the egg yolks and whisk until smooth. While whisking constantly, add the warm vanilla-infused milk, a splash at a time, until blended. When all the milk has been mixed with the egg mixture, pour the combined mixtures into the saucepan.
3. Place the saucepan over medium heat and cook, whisking constantly, until the mixture starts to thicken and bubble. Once you see the first bubbles appear on the surface, set a timer for 1 minute and continue whisking constantly. When the timer goes off, remove the pan from the heat.
4. Put the peanut butter and vanilla into a medium heatproof bowl and set a fine-mesh sieve over the bowl. Pour the hot pastry cream through the sieve, pressing against it with a heat-resistant silicone spatula. Discard any solids in the

CONTINUED

MRS. PUFF'S CREAM PUFFS

CONTINUED

CHOUX PASTRY

½ cup water

½ cup whole milk

6 tablespoons unsalted butter

1 tablespoon sugar

½ teaspoons kosher salt

1 cup all-purpose flour, sifted

4 eggs

CHOCOLATE GLAZE

½ cup heavy cream

Pinch kosher salt

1 cup finely chopped dark chocolate

1 tablespoon dark corn syrup

sieve. Whisk together the pastry cream, peanut butter, and vanilla until well blended and smooth. Cover with plastic wrap, pressing it directly onto the surface of the pastry cream. Let cool for 30 minutes at room temperature, then chill for at least 4 hours. The peanut butter pastry cream can be prepared up to 2 days in advance.

5 Preheat the oven to 400°F. Line a half sheet pan with parchment paper.

6 To make the choux pastry: In a medium saucepan, combine the water, milk, butter, sugar, and salt and bring to a boil over medium-high heat. Remove the pan from the heat, add the flour, and stir vigorously with a wooden spoon or the silicone spatula, making sure to break up any lumps. Continue stirring until the mixture is smooth and lump-free.

7 Return the pan to medium-high heat and continue stirring until the mixture registers 175°F on an instant-read thermometer and starts to pull away from the pan, leaving a film on the bottom. Remove the pan from the heat and transfer the pastry to a stand mixer fitted with the paddle attachment. Mix on low speed until the temperature drops to 145°F (or lower), 1 to 2 minutes.

8 Add the eggs one at a time, beating after each addition until incorporated before adding the next egg and gradually increasing the mixer speed to medium-high. When all the eggs are incorporated, continue to beat on medium-high speed until the batter is a smooth paste.

9 Transfer the choux batter to a piping bag fitted with a ½-inch plain tip. (Or you can spoon the paste into a zip-top plastic bag, secure the top closed, and snip off a lower corner.) Pipe a tiny amount of choux batter under the four corners of the parchment on the sheet pan. This will keep the paper from moving as you pipe the cream puffs.

10 Holding the tip straight down at a 90-degree angle, pipe twelve 2-inch mounds each about 1½ inches tall and spaced

CONTINUED

MRS. PUFF'S CREAM PUFFS

CONTINUED

about 2 inches apart. Pipe slowly so each mound comes out smoothly. Once you get to the correct width and height, stop squeezing the bag and gently twist the piping tip away. Don't worry if a fine tip of batter is left at the top of a mound.

11 When you have finished piping all the mounds, wet the tip of your index finger with water and gently tap the top of each mound to smooth the batter. (At this point, you can shape the mounds more fully with your dampened fingertip, which you may need to do if you used a zip-top bag for piping.)

12 Once the mounds are piped and smoothed, turn down the oven temperature to 375°F and slide the pan into the oven. Bake the pastries until deep golden and puffed, about 30 minutes. Turn off the oven, prop the oven door open with a wooden spoon, and let the puffs slowly cool for another 30 minutes. Then transfer the puffs to a wire cooling rack and let cool completely.

13 Remove the pastry cream from the fridge and whisk until smooth, then transfer to a piping bag fitted with a filling tip (see Notes). One at a time, hold each puff upside down

in your nondominant hand, insert the piping tip into the bottom of the pastry, and pipe in the pastry cream until you barely start to feel the pastry expand in your hand. As each one is filled, place it right-side up on a sheet pan. When all the puffs are filled, loosely tent the pan with plastic wrap or aluminum foil and chill the puffs until serving.

14 To make the chocolate glaze: In a small saucepan over medium heat, warm the cream and salt until simmering. Remove the pan from the heat, add the chocolate, let sit for 1 minute to melt, and then stir until glossy and thick. Stir in the corn syrup (see Notes). Let cool to room temperature.

15 To coat the cream puffs with the chocolate glaze, one at a time, hold each puff by the bottom, dip the top one-third into the glaze, lift out, allow the excess glaze to drip off, and then set the cream puff upright on a serving tray. Serve immediately. These cream puffs are best served the day they are made.

NOTES A filling tip, known as a Bismarck tip, is long and narrow, which allows you to make a small hole and reach deep into the pastry. If you don't have a Bismarck tip, make a small hole with the tip of a chopstick and fit the piping bag with a small plain tip.

If the chocolate glaze splits, is too thick, or looks greasy, add a bit more corn syrup and stir again. Repeat until the glaze looks smooth and glossy but not greasy.

CHAPTER FOUR

DRINKS

DRINKS

You may think that for a community entirely underwater, we wouldn't be thirsty . . . but we are! We've combed through every watering hole, lagoon, saloon, and greasy spoon to find the best of the best.* Each recipe pairs wonderfully with the appetizers and entrées from this cookbook or can be spectacular meals all their own (just ask Larry about his gains thanks to his protein shake).

We were delighted to get not just one but *two* drink recipes from Patrick Star. The first is actually a collab with Squidward, a delicious Ink Lemonade (page 148), now made with zero ink—we swear! The second, Patrick's Pink Punch (page 153), is a light, sparkling beverage made with homemade strawberry syrup. Why, even the mayor created a special drink that she has named the *official* drink of Bikini Bottom. It's called The Bikini Bottom (page 154). Clever, huh?

We're also very excited to present the Kelp Shake 2.0 (page 147) from Mr. Krabs, who promises us that there are no *monstrous* side effects from drinking it. How reassuring! And that's not the only shake you'll find in this book. We've also got The Ultimate Milkshake (page 143) from Captain Frostymug and two different smoothie recipes, one from Sandy Cheeks (page 159) and one from Larry the Lobster (page 158).

We had lots of fun trying all of these drinks from Bikini Bottom's top ten people who were available to come up with drink recipes, and we hope you find something you love in this chapter. Whatever you enjoy drinking, our one wish is this: May you find in the coming pages a pretty potation that tames your thirst, tantalizes your taste buds, and motivates your mind!

* By this we mean the first ten people to submit drink recipes to the official Bikini Bottom Historical Society's Community Cookbook inbox.

THE ULTIMATE MILKSHAKE

CONTRIBUTED BY CAPTAIN FROSTYMUG

Part milkshake, part refreshing limeade, who better to teach us how to make this delightful drink than Captain Frostymug?

Any soda jerk can learn to make a milkshake. I learned how to make this drink while I was traveling up and down the coast of Colombia on my journey to learn the milkshake secrets of the world, and it's all I want in the sweltering summer months! Read on and practice up because there WILL be a test!

SERVES 4

One 14-ounce can full-fat coconut milk

1 cup sweetened condensed milk

Grated zest of 2 limes

Juice of 4 limes

¼ teaspoon kosher salt

2 cups ice cubes

4 lime wheels, for garnish

Whipped cream, for garnish

1. In a blender, combine the coconut milk, sweetened condensed milk, lime zest and juice, salt, and ice and blend on high speed until thick and frosty, about 2 minutes.
2. Divide evenly among four tall glasses. Garnish each glass with a lime wheel on the rim, and whipped cream, and serve immediately.

PINEAPPLE UNDER THE SEA

CONTRIBUTED BY SPONGEBOB SQUAREPANTS

SpongeBob wanted to come up with a drink recipe for this book that reminded him of home, so he took that quite literally and named this bubbly beverage after his house. He writes:

Naturally, it had to have pineapple in it, but I wanted something that felt kinda warm and cozy like snuggling with Mr. Stuffykins, so I added some ginger. It's got lime and pineapple and ginger and bubbles! Ahh, refreshing!

The lime-ginger syrup used in this drink can be made two weeks in advance. We recommend making a double or even triple batch of the syrup. It's great for making this drink, but it's also tasty for making a lime-ginger soda. Just add a tablespoon or two of syrup to a cup of club soda or seltzer, mix, and sip!

SERVES 4

- ½ cup water
- ½ cup sugar
- 1 tablespoon grated lime zest
- 1-inch piece fresh ginger, peeled and thinly sliced
- Ice cubes, for the pitcher
- ¼ cup freshly squeezed lime juice
- 1½ cups pineapple juice
- 2 cups club soda or seltzer
- 4 sprigs mint, for garnish

1 In a small saucepan, combine the water, sugar, lime zest, and ginger and bring to a boil over medium-high heat, stirring until the sugar dissolves. Remove from the heat and let cool for 20 minutes. Strain through a fine-mesh sieve into a small bowl or measuring cup with a spout, cover, and chill for 1 hour.

2 Fill a 1½-quart pitcher about half full with ice. Add the chilled mixture from step 1, the lime juice, and pineapple juice and stir to mix, then top off with the club soda and stir briefly again. Divide among four glasses, garnish each glass with a mint sprig, and serve immediately.

KELP SHAKE 2.0

CONTRIBUTED BY THE KRUSTY KRAB

It wasn't so long ago that everyone in Bikini Bottom was crazy for a Kelp Shake! Even Mr. Krabs' daughter, Pearl, said, "Once you taste the secret goodness of a Kelp Shake, you can't have just one." Unfortunately, drinking Kelp Shakes caused everyone in town to be completely covered in moss-green fuzz. But if there's anything Mr. Krabs loves more than money, it's his daughter. So he invented the Kelp Shake 2.0 just for Pearl. All the green, none of the fuzzies!

SERVES 2

- **1 cup baby spinach leaves**
- **½ cup canned crushed pineapple in juice, undrained**
- **1 teaspoon kelp powder**
- **2 teaspoons blue spirulina powder**
- **1 pint vanilla ice cream**
- **1 to 1½ cups whole milk**

1. In a blender, combine the spinach, pineapple and juice, kelp powder, blue spirulina powder, ice cream, and 1 cup of the milk. Begin blending on low speed, gradually increasing the speed to high and continuing to blend until smooth. If the mixture becomes too thick to blend, turn off the blender, add another ½ cup milk, and then continue blending until smooth.
2. Divide between two cups and serve immediately.

INK LEMONADE

CONTRIBUTED BY SQUIDWARD AND PATRICK STAR

Here's the Patrick and Squidward collab you didn't know you needed! When submitting this recipe, Squidward wanted us to make it very, very clear that this is absolutely *not* made with his ink—that's gross and weird, why would anyone think that? (For the record, we have doubts.) Patrick did contact us later to share the original recipe that may or may not confirm our suspicions, but for this recipe, we chose to use gel food coloring for its distinct black—perhaps . . . inky?—color. Feel free to omit this if you prefer your lemonade ink-free.

SERVES 4 TO 6

1 cup freshly squeezed lemon juice

⅔ cup sugar

¼ teaspoon black gel food coloring, plus more as needed

Ice cubes, for the pitcher

3 cups water

1. In a small bowl, stir together the lemon juice, sugar, and food coloring until the sugar dissolves. Add more food coloring if needed.
2. Fill a 2-quart pitcher about half full with ice. Add the lemon juice mixture and the water and stir to mix. Pour into glasses and serve immediately.

MAYOR

LeMonad

PATRICK'S PINK PUNCH

CONTRIBUTED BY PATRICK STAR

Bright, deep pink, complex, flavorful—most of these are not necessarily words we would use to describe Patrick, who came up with this recipe. This strawberry soda gets layers of flavor from cinnamon, cardamom, and rose water, all of which complement the sweet strawberries. It's one of our favorite drinks in the book, and we couldn't help but wonder how Patrick came up with it. We may never know.

SERVES 6

STRAWBERRY SYRUP

1 pound fresh strawberries, hulled, or frozen strawberries, thawed

1 cup water

1 cup sugar

½ teaspoon ground cardamom

1 cinnamon stick

¼ teaspoon kosher salt

2 teaspoons rose water

TO ASSEMBLE

6 fresh strawberries, for garnish

Ice cubes, for the glasses

6 tablespoons freshly squeezed lime juice

6 cups club soda or seltzer

1. To make the strawberry syrup: In a blender, combine the berries and water and blend until smooth. Strain the puree through a fine-mesh sieve set over a medium saucepan. Discard any solids in the sieve. Add the sugar, cardamom, cinnamon stick, and salt to the saucepan, place over medium heat, and bring to a simmer, stirring frequently. Once the sugar has dissolved, remove the syrup from the heat. Let cool to room temperature, then discard the cinnamon stick. Stir in the rose water, transfer to an airtight container, and chill for at least 1 hour. The syrup will stay fresh in the fridge for up to 1 week.
2. To assemble: First prepare the strawberry garnish. Using a paring knife, and working with one berry at a time, cut from the tip of the berry toward the stem end, extending the cut about halfway through the berry to create a secure cut.
3. To make a drink, fill a pint glass half full with ice. Add 1 tablespoon of the lime juice and ½ cup of the syrup and stir to combine. Top with 1 cup of the club soda and stir gently just until mixed. Garnish with a strawberry on the rim of the glass. Repeat to make five more drinks.

THE BIKINI BOTTOM

CONTRIBUTED BY MS. MAYOR

As fearless leader of the Bikini Bottom Historical Society, I, Ms. Mayor, wanted something that screamed Bikini Bottom, something we could be proud to call our signature drink, something tropical, something fun, something that would encourage you all to vote for me in the next election and cement my position as the most mayoral mayor in Bikini Bottom history! You can bet your sweet bippy that we're going to serve this at every Bikini Bottom Historical Society meeting (and not just because of the Mayoral Decree, though, that was a pretty big contributing factor).

SERVES 6

- 3 cups freshly squeezed orange juice
- 3 cups pineapple juice
- ¼ cup freshly squeezed lime juice
- 2 tablespoons orgeat syrup (see Note, page 157)
- 2 tablespoons grenadine
- 6 fresh pineapple wedges, for garnish
- 6 maraschino cherries, for garnish
- Ice cubes, for the glasses
- Club soda, for topping

1. In a 2-quart pitcher, combine the orange juice, pineapple juice, lime juice, orgeat syrup, and grenadine and stir to mix. Thread a pineapple wedge and a cherry on each of six cocktail skewers.
2. Fill six pint glasses with ice. Fill each glass almost to the top with the juice mixture. Top each glass with a splash of club soda. Garnish with the pineapple-cherry skewers and serve immediately.

FIZZY FANG

CONTRIBUTED BY SLAPPY

This deep-red beverage comes from Nosferatu's servant, Slappy. It's tart, sweet, and fizzy with a strong cherry flavor, and we're just thankful it's not the red beverage we thought it was.

The secret to this tasty beverage? In an interview with Slappy, he said, "I mixed up a batch of this for the boss because I forgot to get his usual supply of blood. He's about to try it for the first time, and I can't wait to hear what he thinks. The excitement is killing me. Is it killing you?"

"Hissss!"

". . ."

"That means he likes it."

SERVES 4

- **4 cups tart cherry juice**
- **¼ cup freshly squeezed lime juice**
- **¼ cup vanilla syrup (see Note)**
- **Ice cubes, for the glasses**
- **2 cups club soda or seltzer**
- **4 lime wheels, for garnish**
- **4 dark cocktail cherries, for garnish**

1. In a small pitcher or a bowl or large measuring cup with a spout, combine the cherry juice, lime juice, and vanilla syrup and stir to mix.
2. Fill four pint glasses with ice. Divide the juice mixture evenly among the glasses and top each glass with ½ cup of the club soda. Garnish each glass with a lime wheel on the rim and a cherry on top. Serve immediately.

NOTE Many grocery stores carry flavored syrups for using with coffee or cocktails. A store-bought syrup works perfectly for this recipe. Feel free to use a sugar-free version.

LARRY'S PROTEIN SHAKE

CONTRIBUTED BY LARRY THE LOBSTER

Finally, the secret to Larry the Lobster's workout routine is revealed and cemented in history so that all may benefit from his knowledge and work toward their own gains and goals! There's a reason he's the lifeguard at Mussel Beach, and this protein shake is the delicious key to his success.

There's nothing I like more than a protein shake before, during, and after a pump sesh! I included berries in this bad boy because of the antioxidants but also to make it match my bright red tannage. The vanilla and fruit are a perfect match, but you could totally use an unsweetened, unflavored protein powder instead. And it's no secret, amigo, that protein powder can help you get j-j-j-jacked!

SERVES 2

2 to 4 scoops vanilla protein powder (see Note)

1 large banana, peeled and cut into thirds

1 cup frozen sliced strawberries

1 cup frozen cherries

2 cups full-fat coconut milk

Few drops of red gel food coloring (optional)

1. In a blender, combine the protein powder, banana, strawberries, cherries, coconut milk, and food coloring (if using). Begin blending on low speed, gradually increasing the speed to high and continuing to blend until smooth, 2 to 3 minutes.
2. Divide the shake between two glasses and serve immediately.

NOTE The serving size for protein powders varies by brand. If one scoop equals one serving, use two scoops. If two scoops equal one serving, use four scoops.

SANDY'S $E = MC^2$ SMOOTHIE

CONTRIBUTED BY SANDY CHEEKS

Not to be outdone, Sandy Cheeks sent in her own protein smoothie:

Now protein ain't just for building muscles. You need it to power your brain too! I happened to make a smoothie just like this when I was trying to help Patrick come up with his own game. That game didn't make a lick o' sense to me, but that doesn't mean the smoothie didn't work.

It wouldn't be a Sandy Cheeks recipe without nuts (except her chili recipe, of course), and this one doesn't disappoint, thanks to a couple of scoops of peanut butter.

SERVES 2

1 to 2 scoops vanilla protein powder (whey or plant based)

1 tablespoon Dutch-processed cocoa powder

½ teaspoon ground cinnamon, plus more for garnish

2 tablespoons creamy peanut butter

1 cup milk (dairy or plant based)

1 cup plain Greek yogurt (dairy or plant based)

1 cup frozen banana slices

1. In a blender, combine the protein powder, cocoa powder, cinnamon, peanut butter, milk, yogurt, and banana slices. Begin blending on low speed, gradually increasing the speed to high and continuing to blend until smooth, 1 to 2 minutes.
2. Divide the smoothie between two glasses. Garnish each glass with a sprinkle of cinnamon and serve immediately.

DIRTY BROKEN GLASS

CONTRIBUTED BY THE SALTY SPITOON

We were a little concerned about this last recipe from The Salty Spitoon because we don't want folks eating broken glass. They've assured us that the "broken glass" in this recipe is just ice. Phew.

This is the regular order from the second toughest customer at The Salty Spitoon, Mrs. Puff. She loves a tall glass of broken glass served in a dirty glass. We recognize that some of you softies might not be so tough, so we altered the recipe for you. We won't tell if you don't.

SERVES 1

Ice cubes, for the glass

1 tablespoon cherry syrup

1 teaspoon vanilla syrup (see Note, page 157)

1 can cola (diet or regular)

2 tablespoons half-and-half

1 Fill a pint glass with ice. Add the cherry syrup and vanilla syrup, followed by the cola. Stir gently to combine, then top with the half-and-half, stirring if desired. Serve immediately.

VARIATION

Ice cubes, for the glass

1 tablespoon pineapple syrup

1 teaspoon vanilla syrup (see Note, page 157)

Juice of 1 lime

One 12-ounce can orange soda (diet or regular)

2 tablespoons half-and-half

1 Fill a pint glass with ice. Add the pineapple syrup and vanilla syrup, followed by the lime juice and orange soda. Stir gently to combine, then top with the half-and-half, stirring if desired. Serve immediately.

CANNED
GREAT TASTE IN A CAN
CORAL

WEENIE
HUT JR's

CLOSING

Now that you've read (and hopefully) cooked your way through this book, we hope you enjoyed each and every one of those recipes as much as we enjoyed putting this book together. This was a very special project for us, getting to go around to all our friends and fellow citizens and ask them for the recipes nearest and dearest to their hearts. It made us proud to be part of the Bikini Bottom community and preserve it for future generations to make and share.

And speaking of community . . . food *is* community. It's how we share a part of ourselves with one another—whether it's a traditional recipe from our culture, something we love that we've tried in our travels, or a family recipe passed down through the generations: Food brings us together. So, we, the Bikini Bottom Historical Society, and all the citizens of Bikini Bottom who've contributed to this book, are glad to have shared our recipes with you and hope that you feel like you're part of the community as well. To that end, in the next few pages, we've included some blank recipe pages for you to record your own recipes.

We thank you for your support, and we wish you many delicious memories!

THE BIKINI BOTTOM HISTORICAL SOCIETY

RECIPE NAME

CONTRIBUTED BY

SERVES

INGREDIENTS

DIRECTIONS

RECIPE NAME

CONTRIBUTED BY

SERVES

DIRECTIONS

INGREDIENTS

RECIPE NAME

CONTRIBUTED BY

SERVES

DIRECTIONS

INGREDIENTS

RECIPE NAME

CONTRIBUTED BY

SERVES

INGREDIENTS

DIRECTIONS

RECIPE NAME

CONTRIBUTED BY

SERVES

DIRECTIONS

INGREDIENTS

RECIPE NAME

CONTRIBUTED BY

SERVES

DIRECTIONS

INGREDIENTS

ACKNOWLEDGMENTS

Thanks so much to my partner, Theo, for being my guinea pig and taste-tester for most of this cookbook, and thanks to our friends for taking all the excess leftovers off our hands. Thanks to Mother Ramsey for clueing me in to the fact that Sand Tarts existed. And thanks to my editor, Dena Rayess, for making this such a fun first project to work on together!

—Jarrett Melendez

Special thanks to Kirsty Cooper, Benjamin Harper, Hannah Harris, Micol Hiatt, Jarrin Jacobs, Amy Jarashow, Risa Kessler, and Raina Moore at Nickelodeon.

INDEX

INDEX

TEN SPEED PRESS
An imprint of the Crown Publishing Group
A division of Penguin Random House LLC
1745 Broadway
New York, NY 10019
tenspeed.com
penguinrandomhouse.com

Typefaces: House Industries' Fink Sans, Latinotype's Garrison, PintassilgoPrints's Mudstone, Resistenza's Pressato, and Mostardesign Type Foundry's Sofia Pro

Library of Congress Cataloging-in-Publication Data
Names: Melendez, Jarrett author. Title: The official SpongeBob SquarePants cookbook: over 50 treasured recipes from under the sea / lovingly collected by the Bikini Bottom Historical Society; recipes developed by Jarrett Melendez. Identifiers: LCCN 2026003647 (print) | LCCN 2026003648 (ebook) | ISBN 9798217273454 hardcover | ISBN 9798217273461 ebook Subjects: LCSH: Cooking LCGFT: Cookbooks Classification: LCC TX714 .M458 2026 (print) | LCC TX714 (ebook) | DDC 641.5—dc23/eng/20260223
LC record available at https://lccn.loc.gov/2026003647
LC ebook record available at https://lccn.loc.gov/2026003648

Hardcover ISBN 979-8-217-27345-4
Ebook ISBN 979-8-217-27346-1

Acquiring editor: Eric Klopfer
Project editor: Dena Rayess
Production editor: Sohayla Farman
Designers: Isabelle Gioffredi and Meggie Ramm
Art director: Emma Campion
Production designers: Mari Gill and Claudia Sanchez
Production: Kelli Tokos
Food photographer: Leela Cyd
Food stylist: Carrie Purcell
Prop stylist: Jaclyn Kershek
Recipe developer: Jarrett Melendez
Copy editor: Sharon Silva | Proofreaders: Rachel Holzman, Miriam Taveras, and Navorn Johnson
Indexer: Ken DellaPenta
Publicists: Maya Bradford and Jennifer Dee
Marketer: Paola Crespo

Manufactured in China

10 9 8 7 6 5 4 3 2 1

First Edition

Cover illustration by Caleb Meurer

The authorized representative in the EU for product safety and compliance is Penguin Random House Ireland, Morrison Chambers, 32 Nassau Street, Dublin D02 YH68, Ireland, https://eu-contact.penguin.ie.